Grab the Brass Ring: The American Carousel

Grab the Brass Ring

The American Carousel

by Anne Dion Hinds

Foreword by Jean M. Auel

Crown Publishers, Inc.,
New York

Published by Crown Publishers, Inc., 201 East 50th Street, New York,
New York 10022

CROWN is a trademark of Crown Publishers, Inc.
Manufactured in Japan

Library of Congress Cataloging-in-Publication Data

Hinds, Anne Dion.
Grab the brass ring: the American carousel/by Anne Dion Hinds.
p.   cm.
1. Merry-go-round art—United States—Collectors and collecting.
I. Title.
NK5033.H56   1990
731'.832—dc20   89-9973
ISBN 0-517-57486-1
Book design by Linda Kocur
10 9 8 7 6 5 4 3 2 1
First Edition

Endpapers: At Prospect Park in Brooklyn, New York, these Carmel horses
impatiently await restoration to their former splendor. Photograph courtesy
Curtis Willocks, Brooklyn Image Group.

Calligraphy courtesy Bernard Maisner.

Photograph credits appear on page 145.

This book is dedicated to Darlene and Tim and Dan;
to the National Carousel Association;
and to all those young and young at heart
who love the old wooden carousels.

Contents

Foreword by Jean M. Auel   viii

Introduction by Frederick Fried   x

Facts and Fantasies   1

The Brass Ring   17

Speaking "Carousel"   24

An Age of Paint and Glitter   38

Dream Makers and Their Toys:
The Carousel Builders   54

Chipping Away at History:
The Carvers and Their Carvings   61

Carousels and Parks, Here and
Gone   87

Music, Music, Music   98

Saving Pieces of Our Past:
Collecting   103

Elbow Grease and Glue:
Restoration   108

Present Plans and Future Fancies   121

Carousel Chronology   130
Carousels and Parks   135
Bibliography   139
Acknowledgments   142
A Guide to the Illustrations   143
Index   146

Foreword

In this wonderful book, full of fact and fantasy, Anne Hinds, both a photographer and a writer, has used her rare combination of talents to remind us of the magic of merry-go-rounds. Not just the fanciful, carved steeds caparisoned in all their finery, often sought by collectors for the works of art they are, but the carousel itself, the magical, musical machine that whirls you off into a world of adventure—or at least conjures up a memory of a time when it did.

Anne Hinds' stunning photographs and lively prose took me back to my first memories of carousels. I remembered Riverview Park on the outskirts of Chicago, and "two-cent day," when two pennies could buy a ticket to all but a few exceptional attractions. A dollar, saved up from lunch money and scrounged from bottle deposits, was enough for streetcar fare to get there, which required two transfers, and back again, a paper cone of cotton candy, and more than twenty-five rides! There were several roller coasters to choose from, plus tilt-a-whirls, ferris wheels, fun houses, and more; but no matter how many other rides were chosen, the day was never complete without at least one whirling adventure on the merry-go-round.

Grab the Brass Ring also brought recollections of Jantzen Beach in Portland, Oregon, and company picnics, when employees and their families had the run of the entire amusement park for the day, compliments of the company. Then it was my children I was taking to ride the merry-go-round. I lifted the youngest up into a saddle that was far too big, while the older ones raced for their favorite ponies before the organ piped up, full of the sound and fury of adventure, as the great machine started its rounds. Watching their expectant faces as the horses began to rise and fall to the thunderous music, I recalled my first merry-go-round ride.

Though Jantzen Beach Amusement Park has disappeared, there are still several carousels in Portland—it is sometimes called the City of Carousels—and I'm delighted. I can still take my grandchildren for a ride on the whirling wheel of adventure and let them experience the magic for themselves. Not many people are as lucky these days.

It saddens me to see a single wooden statue of a carousel horse or menagerie animal in a collection, silently poised to leap, but never moving, and seeming to ache for someone to ease its lonely existence. In a museum or a private home, there is no great machine to bring it to life with furious sound, offering rides to an imaginary world of adventure, and no child, or adult, to clamber on its back. But the grand old carousel is an endangered species. They are not being made anymore, and the merry-go-rounds that are left too often suffer from poor maintenance or are broken up for the collectors of the wooden animals.

Anne Hinds' beautiful book is for all who ever loved carousels, those who have them nearby and those who live in less fortunate places and cannot take a spin back to an earlier time, when adventures could be inspired by a magical machine and imagination. This masterful collection of colorful images and fascinating information may recall old merry-go-round memories, and perhaps inspire the urge to save the ones that are left before this endangered species is gone.

Jean M. Auel
Portland, Oregon

Introduction

In 1959 there were approximately 4,200 operating carousels in the United States. I carried out the survey that uncovered that figure with the enthusiastic cooperation of the International Association of Amusement Parks, the Showman's League of America, and the Guide to American Amusement Parks. Several amusement park publications were most generous, lending free space for my appeal.

Another survey made a few months prior to the publication of this book revealed that there are only 172 operating carousels throughout the country. This shocking statistic suggests that future generations may never experience the aesthetic pleasure of the hand-carved carousel. Unless we all join in the preservation effort, the possibility of the wooden carousel's extinction will be a real one.

The carousel as a work of art was first brought to the attention of the American public in 1964. It was then pointed out that the working carousel contained all the elements of the arts—sculpture, painting, music, and motion. The first museum exhibition of the carousel was at the Museum of Early American Folk Art in New York in 1970 under the title "The Art of the Carousel." I was the curator for that exhibition. The American public since has become aware of the beauty of the carousel and has cherished it as a complete work of art.

However, the title of the exhibition, "The Art of the

Carousel," has been used by plunderers of individual figures off the carousel under the guise of "preserving the art of the carousel"! This has encouraged the dismantling of entire carousels for their "art." The carousel is no longer treated as a romantic and nostalgic amusement, but as *art for profit*.

In 1972, the National Carousel Roundtable was organized; its name was later changed to the National Carousel Association. Its purpose was and is to preserve the hand-carved American carousel. With the formation of this preservation organization, America has been made conscious of its rapidly disappearing heritage, and of the replacement of the wooden carousel by shiny, cold, fiberglass reproductions. The efforts of the NCA's nearly two thousand members have succeeded in rescuing the rides from the auctioneer's grasp.

If the plunderers are not stopped, the number of hand-carved wooden carousels will have been decimated and the already frightening prospect of their complete extinction will have been accomplished. Future generations will need to go to the museums that have preserved the American carousel in its entirety to see what had at one time in the past been a vital part of amusement parks in America.

This book brings back the brighter and lighter side of carousels, their art and their history. It is to be hoped that its subtler message will encourage the survival and joy of the hand-carved wooden American carousel.

Frederick Fried
Lincoln, Vermont

Facts and
Fantasies

*Carousels are magical
fantasy machines upon
which each rider can
spin his or her own web
of dreams. Carousels are
surrounded by mis-
information and legend.
The truth is as exciting
as the folklore, so the
best place to begin is
with a look at both.*

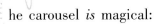he carousel *is* magical:
. . . propelled by band-organ music, haunting or boisterous or
romantic: music to stir your emotions
. . . painted and gilded and jeweled into a dazzling kaleidoscope of vibrant colors
. . . warmed by the twinkling glow and dazzling reflections of
thousands of fairy lights
. . . lit by the enraptured faces of riders old and young.

The merry-go-round can take you on a time-travel ride from
reality to fantasy.

Buy your ticket. Climb aboard. Choose your steed.

The band organ strikes up a wistful tune. The platform begins
to circle. Your horse rises and falls—slowly, unevenly, struggling
against inertia. The ride accelerates. The motion smooths out. Up
and down. Faster and faster. Round and round and round.

The carousel begins to weave its gentle spell. A world of
make-believe drifts into misty focus. Your soaring imagination
spins gossamer dreams you can pursue for a few magical moments.

You are lucky if you live near a park where an old merry-go-
round still spins such magic for you to share with friends and
family. So few are left.

These colorful time machines create a bond of mutual enjoyment among people of all ages. At the century's beginning, they
whirled in parks in every city and town across America. Smaller

Being patient isn't easy. To children waiting to hand over their tickets for Carol's Carousel at the World Forestry Center in Portland, Oregon, it seems to take forever for the ride to end.

Carol's Carousel, Portland, Oregon

Carousel themes are a natural for hot-air balloons. This one welcomed the National Carousel Association conventioneers for an evening at Burlington, Colorado's, P.T.C. #6 in 1984.

portable carousels traveled with every carnival. They were a cherished part of everyone's childhood.

But today the old wooden carousel is an endangered species. During the carousel's Golden Age—roughly 1880 to 1930—at least five thousand hand-carved wooden carousels were built in the United States (there are not enough records to guess more accurately than that). Fewer than 175 are still in existence, fewer than one for every million people.

That's not enough.

And their number continues to dwindle.

Fire, flood, hurricane, or a combination of hard use and too little maintenance have spelled doom for thousands of the carousels that were once a familiar part of the American landscape. And carousels became easy prey to vandals.

Fortunately, owners today are aware that their carousels are valuable antiques. Kept in good repair, the remaining carousels can continue to operate indefinitely for enjoyment and the encouragement of fantasy.

In recent years countless carousels have fallen victim to

Most young girls dream of being princesses. This one surpassed that dream. She became the Junior Rose Queen for the 1986 Portland Rose Festival. She and her court rode the Looff carousel at the Willamette Center.

The center trucks for portable merry-go-rounds were designed to be pulled by horses, later by trucks. Carol's Carousel, Portland, Oregon.

auctioneers, collectors, and dealers who insist that to protect the carvings—the animals, chariots, and decorative panels—they must be put into museums or private collections. A dealer or auctioneer's concern may be swayed by the profit he foresees when he takes down a machine that should stay in operation. A collector may want to possess some rare figure enough to dismantle an entire carousel to obtain it.

Carousel animals should be left on operating machines to be enjoyed by all. The National Carousel Association's former executive secretary, Gail Hall, explains: "A carousel horse off the machine is nothing more than a wooden statue." It comes alive only when it and its companions circle on an operating carousel, carrying happy riders to the music of an old band organ.

That *any* carousels have survived is a tribute to the work of concerned park and carousel owners and organizations such as the National Carousel Association, the Portland-based International Museum of Carousel Art, and the Carousel Society of the Niagara Frontier of North Tonawanda, New York. They are dedicated to keeping the remaining carousels intact and putting idle carousels back into operation. Numerous volunteer groups are working hard, each dedicated to keeping its town's carousel in operation and in tiptop condition. These groups are working, too, to educate the public and to increase awareness of the need to protect for today and for future generations this part of our American heritage.

The antique carousel is mechanically ingenious: a marvel of craftsmanship, a fanciful relic of the gaudy baroque era. Its builders outdid themselves in the creative decoration of wood. The exuberant ornamentation of every available surface with paint, lights, jewels, carving, and mirrors blends deliciously into a spinning swirl of colors.

Will Morton VIII, an art conservator and director of the National Carousel Association, describes the spell an antique carousel can cast: "A carousel is more than just a machine . . . it has been called magical. I think of it as a spiritual dimension—more than just experience, more than just memories."

"Magical" is a word that comes naturally and often to the lips of all those who are in love with the old wooden carousel.

Carousel animals appear to be solid. You might suppose they are carved from a single chunk of wood, but this is true of only a handful of the earliest, most primitive carousels. Even had such huge blocks of wood been available, solid animals would require an impossibly large mechanism to support them and propel their weight. And, because of the characteristics of wood, such carvings

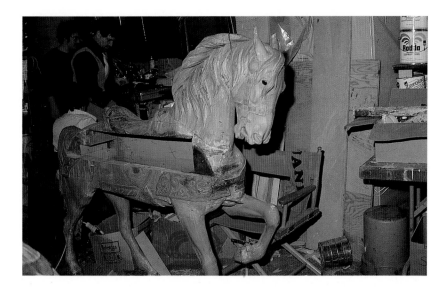

A Muller horse, dismantled for repairs, shows the torso's box construction.

would check and split with every change of weather. Therefore, most carousel animals were built up from slabs—usually two-inch planks—laminated together with rabbit-hide glue to form a hollow box for the torso. The head and legs were assembled separately, then glued and doweled to the body before the final details were carved.

You may hear carousel owners claim that *their* animals are the only ones carved from some exotic wood. Actually, any available hardwood might have been used, but the favorites, the woods most often used because they are fine-grained and easy to carve, were basswood (also called linden), poplar, and yellow pine. Carvers saw extraordinary creatures imprisoned within the wood, creatures more exotic, more alive than their counterparts in zoos or pastures, jungles or barnyards. Deft fingers released from the wood the super-reality of steeds worthy of the riders' innermost dreams; steeds that pulse with vigor, lunging forward even as the carousel stands motionless.

The carvers embellished the muscular bodies with elaborate trappings, often adding wind-whipped banners, colorful garlands, and delicate streamers of ribbon. Behind the saddle or on the horse's shoulder they sculpted faces recognizable from history and mythology. They carved small, familiar animals and strange mythical creatures—winsome or awesome—on saddle cantles. Richly caparisoned armored steeds; patriotically draped military mounts; Indian pinto ponies; cowboy mounts with revolver, lariat, and bedroll—all were designed to attract riders. The "romance side," the side of the animal first seen by the approaching customer, was always more profusely carved and decorated. If jewels were used, they were placed only on the romance side.

After more than a century of carrying riders, the handcrafted

This winsome dapple-gray mare (far right) charms riders on Kit Carson County's P.T.C. #6 at Burlington, Colorado.

wooden carousels have taken on a special magic. If you give them a chance, the animals become as real as they are to the small girl who, one morning just before opening time, circled the merry-go-round and whispered to each wooden horse, "Wake up, horsie." She never doubted that they could hear her.

Such belief, in child or adult, will transform any steed into a creature more than wood, more even than flesh. It becomes the stuff of dreams, ready to carry you off for a joyous romp through the colorful world of the imagination.

Bill Dentzel III has inherited 150 years of family carousel-building tradition. Listen to what he tells an onlooker admiring one of his small, colorful merry-go-rounds: "They're just machines until you get about ten children riding on them. Then they're magical."

With a far-off gaze, he adds, "And the magic is *real*."

As he drives around the United States, the thought comes to him again and again: There aren't enough carousels to put in all the places that need them.

Dentzel postpones the carving of the eyes on his carousel figures until the animal is nearly complete. "It's tricky carving the heads," he explains. "Once you put the eye in, you're dealing with somebody. Until then you can do what you want with them. But once the eye is in, it looks at you."

A spear-carrying hunter peers around the saddle cantle of the zebra on P.T.C. #6 in Burlington, Colorado.

A wealth of folklore has sprung up around the carousel. Many "facts" have been repeated so often that even people within the amusement industry believe them.

On the S&G/Parker carousel at Pueblo City Park in Pueblo, Colorado, a grotesque monkey grins from behind a Parker saddle.

Young girls often talk to the horses and pat them as if they were alive. This large horse with especially ornate trappings is on P.T.C. #84, fondly remembered from its days at Pacific Palisades, New Jersey, and now at Canada's Wonderland, north of Toronto, Ontario.

Carousel-themed floats have become popular in floral parades. This Farmers Insurance float won grand sweepstakes honors in the 1986 Portland Rose Festival Grand Parade.

The giraffe (preceding page) on P.T.C. #6, the Kit Carson County, Colorado, carousel, recalled a childhood incident to one county resident. She told of begging to ride the giraffe just as the family was ready to leave for home after a day at the fair. Her grandmother finally agreed to take her back for a ride and bought the tickets. Then the little girl looked up at the lifelike snake coiled around the giraffe's long neck and burst into tears. She was too scared to ride.

The error persists that the finest American carousels came from Germany. Actually, fewer than a dozen were ever imported. Shipping costs on such bulky freight were enormous. More important, the carvers who could create the most beautifully crafted machines had sought a new life in America.

Most of the talented craftsmen who built these wondrous machines *did* come from Europe. They had spent years in the Old World developing their skills at furniture-making or building wooden ships. One or two had actually worked on carousels before coming to the New World. Emigrating to America, they found in the new, less restrictive land the inspiration to create an exciting new breed of carousel animal. Among this small group of artisans, few had any training in art. Yet when they began to carve carousel horses and menagerie figures, chariots and rounding boards, their hands and eyes took on new and almost mystical abilities. Freed from Old World restraint and pressure to conform, they created more splendid machines and stronger, livelier horses—each with a distinctive personality. This contrasted with the European tradition of populating a carousel with creatures that looked as much alike as possible.

The carousel idea was born in Europe, but it achieved its highest peak of opulence, popularity, and variety in America. Did the legend that American merry-go-rounds were made in Europe arise because of El Dorado, a huge carousel from Leipzig, Germany? One of the very few ever imported to the United States, it ran for many years at Coney Island before being sold in the early 1970s to Toshimaen Amusement Park in Tokyo, Japan.

More confusion arose from the many band organs that *were* imported from Germany, France, and Italy before American factories started producing their own. The band organ's place of origin, emblazoned in gilded letters on its elaborate façade, may have led riders to believe that the entire carousel was imported. Even today, some owners feel there is prestige in claiming Old World origin for their machines, instead of taking pride in their American heritage.

The terms *carousel* and *merry-go-round* mean the same thing, despite claims by some owners that the term depends on the direction the machine rotates, its size, the kind of mechanism that propels it, or whether menagerie animals, in addition to horses, romp on its circular deck.

The location of a carousel shop had some influence on the style of carving done there. The joyful flamboyance of what has come to be known as the Coney Island Style (embodied by Charles I. D. Looff, M. C. Illions, Charles Carmel, Solomon Stein and Harry Goldstein) varies from the dignified realism of the Philadel-

phia Style (Gustav and William H. Dentzel, the Muller brothers, and P.T.C., the Philadelphia Toboggan Company) and the simple practicality of the Country Fair Style (Allan Herschell and his various partners in North Tonawanda, New York, and C. W. Parker in Kansas). Yet the distinction among the styles is often blurred.

The circle traditionally signifies unity, eternity, and wholeness. The Oriental sign for the universe is the circular mandala. A merry-go-round ride may satisfy an instinctive human need for a feeling of continuity or fulfillment.

The experience of a carousel ride usually evokes feelings of serenity, enjoyment, or mystic contemplation. It symbolizes for young and old the festive fun of a holiday, a remoteness from everyday reality, an escape for each rider to a secret world of enchantment.

Strangely, in literature and as a popular expression, the merry-go-round more often symbolizes dark forces or frustration. Ray Bradbury, for example, has woven carousels into several of his dark novels. The carousel in *Something Wicked This Way Comes*, when run backward, can make a rider grow younger, one year for each revolution. The result is less happy than you might expect. In his most recent novel, *Death Is a Lonely Business*, Bradbury sets the action and mood with a carousel in Southern California and describes, as only he can, the destruction of another carousel at a nearby pier.

Down through the ages, circular motion has always had strong

Looff carved only a few prowling tigers. This one hunts aboard the Riverfront Park Carousel in Spokane, Washington.

The kangaroo on the menagerie carousel at Oaks Park, Portland, Oregon, is one of the rarest of the animals that Herschell-Spillman carved.

This ostrich is the only figure saved from the English Chanticleer ride that burned at Dorney Park in Allentown, Pennsylvania, in 1973. When P.T.C. #38 burned there in 1983, only the ostrich on display in the carousel building was saved.

appeal. In his book *The Natural Mind*, Dr. Andrew Weil writes of his findings that spinning provides a natural high. When children discover this phenomenon, they deliberately twirl themselves into a state of euphoria.

Think how many children's games and activities are based on the circle. Watch a small girl fling her arms wide, twirling faster and faster until she collapses in a dizzy heap. Or consider a young boy on a swing: twisting the chains as tightly as he can, he unwinds in a glorious excess of giddy motion. A spin on a carousel excels in producing this exhilarating effect.

Is the Maypole a people-propelled, beribboned ancestor of today's merry-go-round? Its festive colors and bobbing, circular motion may well have inspired a carver to create the first crude carousel.

At Ohio State University, Dr. David Clarke tested a group of young children and found that regular sessions of spinning, by stimulating the inner ears' semicircular canals, can help to develop balance and coordination at an earlier age. And in Burlington, North Carolina, a small carousel built and donated by William H. Dentzel II, the grandson of carousel builder Gustav Dentzel, is being used by the Alamance Developmental Center as a part of its physical therapy program with handicapped children. In ballet, square dancing, and the polka, the heady spin of the dance is the adult version of childhood's prescription for producing giddiness.

The Looff lion (far left) looking outward at the waiting crowd at Port Dalhousie, St. Catherines, Ontario, Canada, is one of only a few of the large and majestic beasts created by the Looff factory.

Four chariot horses, of which this is one, draw the two large chariots on P.T.C. #51 at Elitch Gardens in Denver, Colorado.

In Easton, Pennsylvania,
Bushkill Park's carousel
is filled with the work
of many carvers. This is
a row of winsome
Muller zebras.

The carousel's time-machine effect can whirl you back to your childhood, or even further, to the century's beginning, when the carousel was at the height of its glory and its future throbbed with golden promise.

As the ancient band organ cranks out a familiar tune, it triggers a flood of vivid images. You suddenly find yourself reliving some of childhood's happiest moments. A three-minute ride can stretch into a pleasant, timeless dream; weave a spell of enchantment; or treat you to a glimpse of a glittering future world. A gentle spin on a merry-go-round can launch your imagination on a free-wheeling journey to anywhere. Youngsters gallop into a private world of fantasy. Adults take a nostalgic trip to a less complicated yesterday.

Unfortunately, too many grownups today feel that carousel riding is undignified. They will tell you that "riding the merry-go-round is kid stuff." But you may catch them watching the riders with a wistful expression, as they deny themselves the ageless pleasure of putting a dashing wooden steed through his paces.

When you see a small child almost swallowed up by a huge saddle, you may wonder if carousel makers didn't build with grownup riders in mind. They did. Turn-of-the-century photographs show carousels filled with adults and not a child aboard. Only after amusement parks had become well established were children considered potential customers.

Watch the riders. Children seldom smile as they circle. They wear bemused expressions, unaware of anything beyond their own secret world.

Tiny tots are unpredictable. The more timid ones may burst into sobs the first time they are belted securely onto a saddle. Others chuckle with enjoyment. But most glow with solemn, wide-eyed wonder. Even those who are frightened by the unknown at the beginning of the ride are soon caught up in the music and rhythm and wear tentative smiles by the time the carousel stops. Some overcome their fears so rapidly that they insist on another ride at once. More than one small rider has been persuaded to relinquish a favorite steed only after being told by the operator, "The horse needs a rest. You can come back and ride another time."

If you watch carousels for any length of time, you are sure to witness this scene. It enacts a common ritual: The carousel is ready to start. A young couple, the man carrying a tiny baby, climb aboard. The woman mounts a horse. The man hands the

blanketed child up to her, and swings astride the next steed. Both parents watch the sleeping baby lovingly throughout the ride. As they leave, their faces glow with the knowledge that they have introduced their newborn to an important experience.

Some riders, as they circle, crane their necks to peer straight upward at the mechanism which gives the animals their galloping motion. Others look inward at the band organ or the flashing reflections in the center panel mirrors. Some, peering outward, may seem to be watching the world spin by. But for all of them, reality has for the moment ceased to exist. They are lost in a delicious time warp of imagination. And that is what riding a carousel is all about.

The Brass Ring

If you spent your childhood in an urban setting, your memories will be of the large, elaborately decorated carousel you rode in the city park or nearby amusement park. That carousel probably had a ring machine. Part of the ride's fun was the challenge of catching the brass ring for a free ride.

But if you lived in a rural area, your rides would more likely have been on the portable merry-go-rounds that traveled the fair or carnival circuit. In that case, the ring machine may not have been part of your childhood. Not many youngsters today get a chance to compete for the brass ring. This exciting added attraction to the carousel ride has almost vanished. There are ring machines on fewer than a dozen carousels today throughout the United States and Canada. The stratospheric cost of liability insurance has retired the rest.

Winning a free ride for snagging the coveted brass ring is only part of the fun of the ring machine. You feel a thrill of triumph when you catch any ring. Another comes when you gain enough skill to pitch it accurately into the waiting receptacle.

The connection between the brass ring and the horse has its roots in antiquity. In his book *A Pictorial History of the Carousel*, Frederick Fried tells how Moorish and Arabian horsemen in the 10th century developed their skills with the lance: they practiced by spearing a ring that was suspended from a tree or post. The best of them could do it riding at a full gallop. This test of skill became

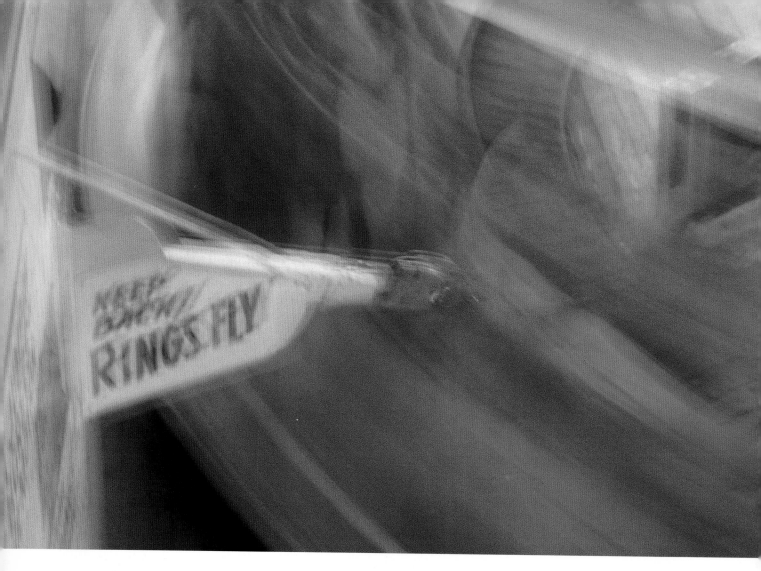

The Flying Horses of Martha's Vineyard, Massachusetts, is one of the country's oldest carousels. The sign on its ring machine warns: "Rings Fly."

part of the great European tournaments known in France as *carrousels*; they were staged by royalty beginning in the 17th century.

The first carousel as we know it was conceived late in that century. Noblemen practiced so hard for the *carrousel* they overworked their horses. That compelled some clever inventor to devise a wheel-like contraption novice lancers could ride during practice. The lancers sat on wooden horses or in chariots suspended from the wheel. The wheel was mounted flat atop a pole and pulled in a circle by a workhorse.

Carousel owners and operators Duane and Carol Perron of Portland, Oregon, own several ring machines. The Perrons would be delighted to be able to install them on their operating carousels. However, the prohibitive cost of insurance has kept their ring machines in storage. They will eventually be put on display in the International Museum of Carousel Art as artifacts of a bygone time.

The management of Sea Breeze Park on Lake Ontario at Irondequoit Bay, Rochester, New York, figures that every year between 1962 and 1972 they replaced more than a ton of metal

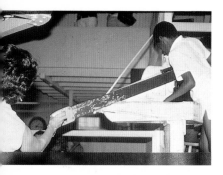

The operator at the Flying Horses of Martha's Vineyard, Massachusetts, feeds additional rings into the machine's arm, as a rider leans out in the hope of catching the gold one.

Attorney William Dentzel II, grandson of Gustav Dentzel, carries on the family tradition by building kiddie carousels. He designed this appealing fish-mouth ring machine for his small merry-go-rounds.

rings. Some riders took the rings home as souvenirs of a special day, but others tossed them through the windows of park buildings or caused other damage with them. The costs of damage and ring replacement were high for that park, like many others.

Finally, in 1972, Sea Breeze's insurance company strongly recommended removing the ring machine, pointing out that the park could be the target of a large lawsuit if someone were injured while reaching for a ring. Sea Breeze reluctantly complied, and a long-standing tradition died, mourned by thousands of loyal riders.

A few carousels do still offer the challenge of catching the ring. The owners of the Santa Cruz Beach Boardwalk carousel removed their ring machine during World War II, because they couldn't get metal rings. Loud protests from disappointed riders brought it back after the war. You can still catch a brass ticket to a free ride there. The boardwalk must replace twenty thousand per

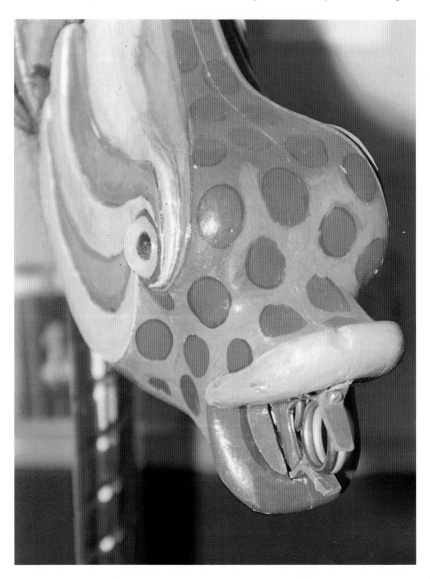

A lively armored horse with a unicorn horn rides the Herschell-Spillman carousel at Balboa Park, San Diego.

The ring this boy on the Spokane Looff has just caught is not metal but plastic, a concession to the high cost of replacing rings.

Carol's Carousel, Portland, Oregon.

The ring machine at Gillian's Fun Deck in Ocean City, New Jersey (far right), before the merry-go-round was broken up and sold.

year of these popular though unauthorized souvenirs.

Mention carousels to anyone who lived as a child in Spokane, Washington, and you will be treated to a tour of that person's memories of the city's special carousel, an elaborate, historic Looff. Adult riders race children in a frantic dash for the outside-row horses so they can compete for the brass (now plastic) ring. If the children aren't fast, they don't stand a chance.

Perhaps if all carousels had ring machines, grownups in other parts of the country would be less hesitant to ride.

You will still find a ring machine at the country's second-oldest merry-go-round, the "Flying Horses" of Watch Hill, Westerly, Rhode Island. Old-timers will recount for you their memories of earlier times when each horse was equipped with a small scabbard holding a wooden rapier for spearing a ring. The rapiers' roots go back to the centuries-old challenge of noblemen spearing the ring in order to perfect their jousting skills.

Jousting tournaments have been a long-time tradition in several parts of the country. In Cordova, on Maryland's Eastern Shore, the Old St. Joseph's Jousting Tournament has been an

annual event since 1868. The contest of spearing a ring from a charging horse was "modernized" in 1917, when contestants took to riding automobile fenders instead of horses. There was no romance in that, and the idea—and the tournament—died with World War I. The original horseback contest was revived after the end of that war.

Since colonial times the Middleton Lancing Tournament has been a tradition of the aristocratic country life at Middleton Place, a plantation near Charleston, South Carolina. Each year costumed horsemen compete at "tilting the rings" to an admiring audience of ladies wearing the garb of colonial times.

Catching the brass ring has long been a symbol of good luck, a symbol that will continue long after the last ring machine has been relegated to a museum, and the origin and meaning of the phrase has been forgotten.

Ring Machines in Operation

Note: These ring machines may not be working at the time you visit. Most are operated only at certain times of the day.

California
•

San Diego Balboa Park: Herschell-Spillman, 1912, three-row menagerie

Santa Cruz Santa Cruz Beach Boardwalk: Looff, 1910, four-row

Massachusetts
•

Martha's Vineyard Oak Bluffs Flying Horses: C. W. F. Dare, pre-1884, two-row

New Jersey
•

Ocean City Wonderland Pier: P.T.C. #75, 1926, three-row

New York
•

Baldwin Nunley's Carousel: Murphy/S&G, 1910–1912, three-row

Coney Island, Brooklyn B & B Carousel: Carmel (no date), three-row

Pennsylvania
•

Easton Bushkill Park: Long /Muller/Dentzel/Carmel, 1903, three-row menagerie

Elysburg Knoebels Amusement Resort: Kramer's Carousel Works/Carmel, c. 1913, three-row

Pen Argyl Weona Park: Dentzel, c. 1917, three-row

Rhode Island
•

Watch Hill Watch Hill Flying Horses: Dare, c. 1884, two-row

Washington
•

Spokane Riverfront Park: Looff, 1909, three-row

The language of the carousel world is a color-ful mixture of "carny"— or carnival—talk, a smattering of 19th-century America, a bit of British, a touch of French, and a few words exclusive to the carousel. All stirred together, they paint a visual image of the machine dedicated to our most creative fantasies.

Speaking "Carousel"

I don't care *what* the sign says," you overhear the gray-haired man say vociferously as he stands watching his grand-children circle on the colorful machine. "That's not a carousel."

"Oh? What is it, then?" challenges his companion.

"It's a merry-go-round," replies the first with authority. "Carousels have all sorts of animals, like lions and tigers and cats and dogs. But a merry-go-round only has horses. That's why this one's a merry-go-round, not a carousel. That sign is *wrong*."

Don't try to correct him. He's positive he's right. That distinc-tion is made so often, even by carnival and amusement park people, that someday it will probably become a dictionary-approved difference. But for now, dictionaries and carousel buffs agree: both words mean the same thing. *Merry-go-round* is an American term. It has been around for a long time to describe the familiar amusement park ride. The word *carousel* was imported from France during the American carousel's Golden Age, when a more elegant name was needed for those large confections of color and light that were centerpieces in parks all across the country. "*Le Grande Carrousel*" (sic) sounds more impressive, more likely to attract adult riders. But either term is correct.

Carrousel, the French word for "tournament," came originally from the Italian. It could have been derived from any of four Italian words: *carosello*, "a ball game"; *carrosello*, the diminutive of *carro*, which means "chariot"; *garrosello*, "little war"; or *garusello*, the

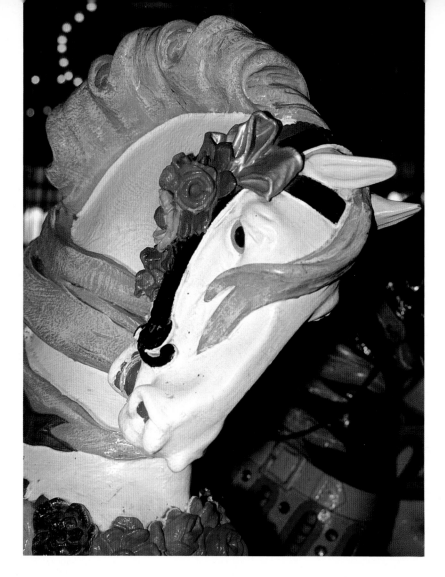

Dragon Chariot, Crescent Park Carousel (preceding page), East Providence, Rhode Island.

A head on the Illions carousel at Riverside Park in Agawam, Massachusetts, before its recent restoration. Fewer than half a dozen pure Illions carousels run today.

Merrick Price, vice-president of Sea Breeze Park, Rochester, New York, enjoys riding on other carousels than his park's P.T.C. #36. Here he takes a spin on the Dutch carousel at Edaville Railroad, South Carver, Massachusetts.

■

name for a clay ball, literally "little head" (because of the ball's resemblance to a bald pate), and for a game played on horseback with a perfumed clay ball, whose breaking marked the scent-drenched horseman it hit as the loser.

A dozen creative variations of the spelling of carousel appeared on the shop signs and letterheads of carousel builders of seventy-five years ago. Many builders were inconsistent in their spelling over the years. "Carousel," the simplest spelling and probably the most accepted, will be used throughout this book.

Kinds of Carousels

■

A *menagerie*, or *menagerie carousel*, has on board many other animals besides horses. Often names designate a specific mechanism design. *Flying Horses* were early carousels whose crude steeds were suspended from an overhead wheel—similar to another amusement park ride, the *flying swings*. The horses, which swung outward by centrifugal force as they spun, needed no platform underneath.

A griffon chariot on
the Parker carousel at
Lakeside Park in
Denver, Colorado.

At Watch Hill, Rhode Island, you can still see Flying Horses
in operation. That primitive machine is listed on the National
Register of Historic Places. It is so fragile that only children are
allowed to ride it, so you will have to be content with watching the
younger generation circle.

Allan Herschell built his first portable *steam riding gallery* in
1883. It was up-to-date for its time, for it ran on a track and was
belt-driven by a large steam engine located a distance from the
carousel. The design gained instant popularity.

Some early names of carousels still heard occasionally in
rural America are *Flying Jenny* (or *Jinny)* and *Spinning Jenny*, all
flying horses. On *track machines* the animals are propelled from
underneath. The early Parker Carry-Us-All and some early Her-
schell-Spillmans were track machines: small, usually with two
rows, and steam-powered. Much larger—and faster—variations of
the track machine are the racing derby and the steeplechase.

After placing the truck assembly, raising the center pole, and putting up the sweeps, the next project is to haul up the heavy canvas canopy.

The quarter-poles brace the canopy above the sweeps. 1978 was the first year this novice volunteer crew put up the carousel at the Forestry Center in Portland, Oregon.

This Stein & Goldstein dapple-gray horse with roses (far right) is a favorite on the recently restored S&G/Parker mixed carousel at Pueblo City Park, Pueblo, Colorado.

In Great Britain, *roundabout* (originally a term describing a system of plowing) is more commonly heard than *carousel*. A carousel there may also be called a *whirligig* or *galloper*. The Spanish call it either *caballitos* ("little horses") or *tío vivo*, a charming term that translates to "lively uncle." Germans call it *das Karussell*; the Norwegians, *karusell* or *rundkjoring*. In French it is not *carrousel*, as you might expect, but *manège de chevaux de bois*, "riding school of wooden horses." Japan has two names: *kaitan mobuka*, "rotating wooden horse," and the Americanized *merigo-raundo*.

Carousels designed for permanent installation at one location, usually an amusement park, are designated *park machines* or *permanent machines*. Some, however, have been moved many times from one park to another, often clear across the country. These large and ornate machines are almost always housed in a building. At the very least, they are protected by a roofed, open-sided gazebo. Park machines usually are three- or four-row (or *-abreast*), counted from the outer edge to the center. A few five- and six-row machines were built. Park machines may be as much as 65 feet in diameter, although the more common range is between 40 and 50 feet. A *stationary* carousel is one with no jumping animals.

Cedar Point's rare Racing Derby, 90 feet in diameter and four abreast, is one of only two still operating. The other is at Rye Playland in Rye, New York. They give a very fast ride, with the added thrill of a race: the horses in each row compete against each other.

Portable carousels, usually two- or three-abreast, are smaller and less elaborate. They were designed for quick assembly and easy portability in traveling carnivals and fairs. They were moved every few days during the carnival or fair season, so the emphasis in their design was on ease of handling.

Allan Herschell, William F. Mangels, and M. C. Illions manufactured *kiddie carousels:* simple merry-go-rounds, usually two-row, for very small children. The horses were generally made of cast metal instead of wood, although one beautiful Illions-made wooden one operated at Shady Lake, Ohio, until a few years ago.

Most of the old portable machines, worn out by hard use, have disappeared. A few have found their way into city parks or amusement parks, where they have been restored and permanently installed.

Related Rides

■

Many rides that are not carousels in the strict sense are similar enough that you should know about them. The *Steeplechase,* which gave its name to one of Coney Island's famous parks, had horses similar to those found on a merry-go-round. Carrying two riders each, they ran on a track that circled the roof outside the park's huge main building. Riders could experience the thrill of a race while enjoying a panoramic view of the entire park from a heart-stopping height and speed. A revival of Steeplechase Park, now in the planning stages, will feature the well-remembered steeplechase ride.

Another rare ride is the *racing derby.* The firm of Prior & Church, Santa Monica, California, built a few of these, usually with Illions- or Looff-carved horses. The horses, each saddled for two riders, give a breathtakingly fast ride on a large circular track, with a mechanism designed to allow first one, then another of the horses in a row to pull out ahead. Two of the finest and largest ever made were four-abreast machines 90 feet in diameter. They are still favorite rides at Cedar Point in Sandusky, Ohio (formerly at Euclid Beach, near Cleveland) and at Rye Playland, in Rye, New York.

A close relative of the carousel was operated for many years at Opryland, U.S.A., in Nashville, Tennessee. It was recently donated to the Historical Amusement Foundation to be installed in that group's planned old-fashioned amusement park in Morgantown, Indiana. That *rolling gondola* has eight large rocking carriages instead of horses. It was reputedly built in Germany's Black Forest, discovered in five thousand unmarked pieces in a Danish barn, and brought to Nashville, where it was reassembled with only an old postcard as a guide.

Carvings

■

The animals on the earliest carousels were attached solidly to the platform and did not go up and down as they circled. Some early carousels did have animals that swung, suspended by chains from overhead. It was not until Frederick Savage of England invented the *jumping*, or *galloping*, *mechanism* in about 1880, that the ride became more exciting—more like riding a live horse.

Even when inside rows of animals move up and down, those on the outside row are often stationary. Called *standers*, with three legs fastened to the deck, they are the largest figures on the carousel. They may be horses or other kinds of beasts. Carvers let their imaginations soar when they created the outside row, for it is the first to catch your eye as you approach the carousel. These show animals were not only the most elaborately carved, but also the most vividly painted. They are, however, the least popular to ride because most people prefer the jumpers.

The *lead horse*, or *king horse*, is traditional on park machines. It is the most ornately carved, has the finest of trappings, and serves as the marker for the ticket-taker collecting ride tickets. The lead horse is often armored or elaborately festooned with flowers, and is always a favorite with riders. The inner rows of animals are usually *jumpers*. They are suspended in midair as if going at a full gallop. More rare are *prancers*, whose hind legs stand on the deck while their forelegs paw the air. Horses were occasionally carved as prancers, the most popular pose for cats, frogs, goats, rabbits, and dragons.

The first ride on Carol's Carousel that first year was a satisfying achievement for owner Duane Perron.

Carol's Carousel, Portland, Oregon.

■

31

One of the finest and most detailed of all carousel carvings—the armored Muller anniversary horse—is on the Kiddieland Dentzel/Muller carousel at Cedar Point in Sandusky, Ohio. The horse appears on one of the four United States carousel stamps issued in 1988.

The Mother Goose figure from a rare Allan Herschell "Blue Goose" kiddie ride, owned by Carol and Duane Perron, Portland, Oregon. Only two are known to exist. The other is at Waldameer Park in Erie, Pennsylvania. These small, one-row rides, designed for children, have winsome goose and pelican figures.

In addition to the animals on a carousel, *chariots*, sometimes called *sleighs*, are provided for those who don't want to climb up on a lively steed. Large carousels may carry from two to four massive chariots, each with two or three benches, occasionally wide enough to seat five people across. The sides of the chariots provided carvers with large expanses of wood to decorate, inspiring them to extravagant ornamentation. Whatever the carver saw in the wood he carved and embellished lavishly, with dragons, cupids, lovers, swans, or figures from history and mythology.

Parker, Herschell-Spillman, and a few other manufacturers also offered *lovers' tubs,* or *flying tubs:* revolving circular tin seats, upholstered and decorated. You can still ride in these tubs at Oaks Park in Portland, Oregon, and on the Pueblo City Park Carousel in Pueblo, Colorado. You can either ride in leisurely circles or make them spin with giddying speed, rotating in a smaller circle as the carousel goes around.

The *romance side* of an animal or chariot faces outward on the carousel. It is more intricately carved and jeweled than the inner side. In America, carousels rotate counterclockwise, so the riders on the outside row can more easily reach for the brass ring. Thus, the right side is the romance side. In Great Britian the romance side is on the left. There, machines rotate clockwise, so riders can mount their chosen steeds from the "proper" side.

Music

∎

A *band organ* often provides the music for carousels. This sophisticated instrument is housed in a handsomely decorated case that may be carved and gilded. Operating drums, cymbals, and trumpets may be visible on its façade. An animated figure of a band conductor directs the music on some of the more elaborate models. The carousel band organ is often mistakenly called a *calliope.* The calliope is actually a much simpler instrument whose sounds come from a series of loud, shrill steam whistles. The band organ is operated by compressed air, and uses paper rolls similar to piano rolls, or folded "books," or some other mechanical method of reproducing the familiar carousel music.

The Mechanism

■

The *truck assembly* is the drive mechanism in the center of the carousel, from which the rest of the machine is suspended and propelled. The name originated in the early days when the unit was towed from place to place by a horse or tractor. With the coming of the steam engine for driving power, the truck assembly became self-propelled. Today, it is towed by a truck.

The *center pole* is a part of the truck assembly. It is the upright post from which the entire carousel is suspended; the carousel is hung from the *main bearing* on which it rotates. The horizontal *sweeps* (called swifts in England) radiate from a *bevel gear* and are supported by the *sweep stay rods. Drop rods* extending down from the sweeps hold up the *platform*, or *deck*.

The *canopy*, or *canvas*, is hung from the top of the mast that extends above the center pole. It is kept taut by the *quarter poles* and looks like a giant umbrella. The canopy gives needed protection from the weather to portable machines but is unnecessary for

A small Parker lovers' tub spins on the S&G/Parker carousel at Pueblo City Park in Pueblo, Colorado.

An unusually large rocking chariot is popular with riders on the ornate Herschell-Spillman menagerie carousel that spins just outside the zoo entrance at Balboa Park in San Diego, California.

■

33

A grinning jester-head shield on the carousel at Kennywood in West Mifflin, Pennsylvania, is typical of the shields on Dentzel carousels.

permanent ones installed in buildings.

Rounding boards, or *crestings*, often lighted by hundreds of light bulbs, cover the outside edge of the canopy and sweeps. *Shields* conceal the edges of the rounding boards. *Center panels* may cover only the top part of the drive mechanism. On larger and fancier machines, you may find center panels enlarged to form a housing that surrounds the entire workings and supports. Most center panels feature wood-framed oil paintings on stretched canvas, or mirrors, or both, and lights to add dazzle.

Carvers

■

The *carvers* were the craftsmen who designed and carved the carousel animals, chariots, and other decorative wooden parts. When the industry was young, the carvers were often the manufacturers as well. Carousels are frequently called by the surname of the factory's master carver or owner: *Looff, Dentzel, Stein & Goldstein,* or *Illions,* for example.

Other carousels are named for the manufacturer. The *Philadelphia Toboggan Company* ("toboggan" here refers to an early style of roller coaster), usually abbreviated to *P.T.C.,* gave each of its machines a number. That has made it easier to track the history of P.T.C. carousels through the years and to document the moves they have made from park to park and from city to city.

Restoration

∎

Restoration is the process of returning a carousel as nearly as possible to its original condition. Some carousels are regularly painted and repaired so they do not require complete restoration. George Long, the late owner of Sea Breeze Park, once said proudly of his P.T.C. #36 that it never needed restoration because "it is always kept in good order." Long's granddaughter, Susan Price Hofsass, has nearly completed restoration of the carousel's horses to their original colors.

Original paint was that which was applied at the factory at the

Carol's Carousel, Port-land, Oregon.

The center panels at the Balboa Park Herschell-Spillman menagerie in San Diego, California, still have their original paint.

∎

35

Street merry-go-rounds, mounted on trucks, were magnets for children in America's large cities. This one and its truck was restored by Will Markey, Dallastown, Pennsylvania.

time the carousel was built. It may include realistic tones for the body; brilliant colors for the trappings; stenciled or hand-painted decorative detailing, striping, gilding, and shading; and gold or other metal leaf. Not many carousels today wear their original paint. A rare example of one on which you can see the elegance of the finest original paint is the Kit Carson County, Colorado, machine, P.T.C. #6, restored by careful cleaning and retouching by artist Will Morton VIII.

Factory paint was that which was added when a carousel was returned to the factory for repairs, updating, or restoration.

Park paint is the glossy enamel used on animals that are to be placed on an operating carousel. When the animal is to be displayed in a home or office, a matte finish, sometimes antiqued, is often preferred.

Parks

■

The old-fashioned amusement park with its rides strung along a midway or grouped in a circle is called a *traditional park*. Lakeside Park in Denver, Colorado, which opened in 1908; turn-of-the-century Palace Playland in Old Orchard Beach, Maine; and

Lagoon, in Farmington, Utah, which dates from the 1800s, are classified as traditional parks.

Disneyland opened in 1955 as the world's first *theme park*. Theme parks are divided into sections, each with a different historic, geographic, or storybook theme. Many of the new theme parks have bought historic carousels, restored them, and put them into operation. Six Flags Over Georgia rescued P.T.C. #17 from storage after the closing of Chicago's Riverview Park. It takes great pride in the historic significance of that splendid machine, which is housed in a building that duplicates its Riverview home.

Charles J. Jacques, Jr., in his *Amusement Park Journal*, devised a new category for parks: the *hybrid park*, which has the features of both the traditional and the theme park. Cedar Point in Sandusky, Ohio, which tops the nation in number of rides, is an outstanding hybrid park, with a traditional midway and several themed areas.

Trolley parks were those built by the traction companies at the end of their streetcar line. They flourished around the turn of the century. Many survive, but the streetcar tracks have probably been torn up to make room for a highway to the park.

P.O.P., or pay-one-price, is the admission system at most theme parks and at some of the traditional ones. The payment of an entrance fee entitles the visitor to unlimited rides. Other parks charge little or no entrance fee but require a ticket purchase for each ride. The term *P.O.P.* may have had its origin in the nickname "P.O.P." given to Pacific Ocean Park in Santa Monica, California. That park opened in 1950 as Ocean Park and was updated with a marine theme in 1958. Numerous problems beset the park: it was an idea ahead of its time; the P.O.P. tickets were priced too low to pay for proper maintenance; the Southern California climate allowed the park to remain open all year, which made maintenance difficult; the park's location on a pier that extended into the surf exposed the rides to the corrosive effect of the salt air. The park deteriorated rapidly and closed, bankrupt, in 1968.

The language of the carousel, as you can see, is every bit as colorful as the wonderful machines it describes.

The Golden Age of the Carousel spanned the half-century between 1880 and 1930, when most of the great wooden carousels were created. Before that, human beings had spent thousands of years discovering the joys of spinning in circles.

An Age of Paint and Glitter

S team power. The billowing clouds of water vapor signaled a revolution of gigantic proportions. Steam power brought changes to America that forever altered the country's face. It set off massive movements of population from country to city and from east to west. It generated rapid growth in the manufacture of consumer goods. And it significantly increased leisure time for the working classes.

It all began in the 19th century, when steam replaced wind to propel ships, and steam locomotives took over the burden of the long haul from the horse and wagon. Waterways and rails criss-crossed the country, opening up vast new lands to settlement. A dramatic drop took place both in manufacturing and transportation costs and in the time it took to move people and goods.

At the same time, the steam-powered tractor cut drastically the need for farmhands. One man could now do the work that had required a crew of laborers. Workers displaced by the chuffing monsters moved to towns and cities to find jobs in factories. There, steam power increased productivity, allowing shorter working hours. Members of the working class found themselves with some-thing they had never known before: leisure time.

And what has all of this to do with the carousel?

Everything.

No longer was the brute strength of a man or a horse needed to turn a merry-go-round. Steam power made it possible for those colorful rides to become larger, carry more people, and bring in

more revenues. Thus began the half-century, from about 1880 to 1930, of "The Golden Age of the Carousel."

Our remote ancestors most likely used spinning in circles as a form of entertainment. In medieval Europe, where tournaments were staged as competitions in knightly prowess, slaves or serfs were exploited to turn crude merry-go-rounds for the enjoyment of their wealthy and aristocratic masters. It was not until the steam engine came into common use that the carousel could become a practical device for entertaining the masses.

During the 19th century, the pleasure gardens that had been popular in Europe for several hundred years gradually evolved into amusement parks. The idea made the ocean voyage to America, where it took root in fertile ground and grew rapidly. Amusement parks soon outstripped their European ancestors in size and diversity.

The exact moment of the carousel's beginning in America is lost to history. The merry-go-round and the amusement park were too much taken for granted for the details of their birth or growth to have been recorded. However, primitive carousels must have been around earlier than 1784: that year the New York City Common Council passed a law banning them as dangerous.

As the iron-hulled ship replaced the wooden sailing vessel, shipwrights turned their skills to carving carousel figures. They were joined by carvers who emigrated to "The Land of Opportunity" from Europe. Many who came to America to ply their trade of furniture making discovered carousel carving to be lucrative and challenging. Few of these craftsmen had any formal training in art, yet their sculptures in wood became, according to *The Treasury of American Design*, "works of art in their own right."

With the development of steam power and the invention of the jumping mechanism in 1880 by Frederick Savage of King's Lynn, Norfolk, England, carousel rides became more realistic: the animals galloped up and down in addition to going around and around.

The amusement park business began in earnest just before the turn of the century when the trolley park caught on in America. Looking for additional income from weekend fares, someone at one of the traction companies was struck with an innovative idea: Why not build a park at the end of a streetcar line? The destination was a bucolic spot that offered a body of water for bathing, a place to picnic, and paths for strolling through shady green countryside. Other trolley companies adopted the idea, and city dwellers, remembering their rural ancestry, thronged to the parks for weekend outings. Soon, playgrounds, food booths, and bandstands were added to lure customers.

This colorful steam engine (preceding page) still operates the elaborate portable Savage roundabout at Great Adventure.

Louise Muller Reyes, Daniel Muller's daughter, tells her haunting version of the legend long woven into the mystique of the ornate Frontier Town carousel, one of five at Cedar Point in Sandusky, Ohio: "At midnight a lady comes out to visit the horses, and when she rides Blackie the lights and the music of the carousel come on and it starts up. That lady is my mother, who died when I was nine months old."

The trolley that once took fun-seekers to Council Crest Amusement Park in Portland, Oregon, now gives rides around the Oregon Electric Railway Museum grounds in Glenwood, Oregon.

Carousels Operating in Their Original Locations

California
•

Santa Cruz Beach Boardwalk, Santa Cruz: Looff, c. 1910, four-row; ring machine

Colorado
•

Elitch Gardens, Denver: P.T.C. #51, 1920–1928, four-row

Maryland
•

Glen Echo Park, Glen Echo: Dentzel, 1921, three-row menagerie

New Jersey
•

Clementon Lake Amusement Park, Clementon: P.T.C. #49, 1919, four-row

New York
•

George F. Johnson Rec Park, Binghamton: Allan Herschell, 1925(?), four-row

Ross Park Zoo, Binghamton: Allan Herschell, c. 1920, four-row

George W. Johnson Park, Endicott: Allan Herschell, c. 1923, three-row

C. Fred Johnson Park, Johnson City: Allan Herschell, c. 1923, four-row

West Endicott Park, Union: Allan Herschell, 1929(?), three-row

Business boomed when park owners began to provide customers with amusements in which they could participate, instead of merely being spectators: rides, shooting galleries, skating rinks, and dance floors became the parks' big attractions.

The first ride to be installed in a trolley park was usually a merry-go-round, a powerful magnet for fun-seeking customers. As other rides were added, the carousel became the hub of the park, the glittering center from which the other amusements radiated.

Steam-propelled rides were a great improvement over the earlier man- or horse-drawn ones, but they were dirty and noisy. There was no question about it: further improvements were needed. When the electric trolley companies tapped into their electric lines for clean, plentiful power for the carousel, it became still larger, able to accommodate more riders, more ornate, and brilliantly lit. Electric power also allowed the design of other bigger, faster, and more complex amusement rides.

By the turn of the century, the amusement park was an exciting urban successor to such rural social activities as the husking bee, the barn raising, and the country fair. You can still take a nostalgic trip to the past by visiting one of the surviving trolley parks. Many that were once shady oases far out beyond the city are encircled by urban growth.

Riverside Park at Agawam, Massachusetts; Sea Breeze, on Lake Ontario near Rochester, New York; Oaks Park in Portland, Oregon; and Kennywood, near Pittsburgh, Pennsylvania, are among the hundreds of trolley parks that blossomed at the end of a streetcar line or an interurban railway.

Later, many parks were sold by the traction companies to cities or private operators. New rides were always in demand. Carousel mechanism builder William F. Mangels invented the Whip, and George Tilyou of Coney Island designed the human roulette wheel. Roller coasters, which had been around since before the Civil War, grew larger and faster, becoming huge skeletons that proclaimed the location of a park from a distance.

Rides, especially those that gave the feeling of danger and bravado, grew in number and complexity. The merry-go-round became the ride for the very young, the less brave, and those who had had their fill of being tossed around and terrified.

The business of carousel making in America began when individual carvers—often furniture makers by trade—created machines in their spare time. Those who found they could run their carousels at a profit went into the manufacturing business full time, hiring carvers and expanding their operations as the market for their creations grew.

By 1900 more than a dozen shops had sprung up in Brooklyn

and North Tonawanda, New York; in Philadelphia, Pennsylvania; and in Abilene, Kansas. In Abilene, teenager Dwight D. Eisenhower is reputed to have had a summer job sanding horses. The first handful of builders had difficulty keeping up with the demand from carnivals for the simple portable merry-go-rounds and from amusement parks and city parks for the large, elaborate machines they needed for the right touch of glitter, fun, and fantasy. The large carousels, although they looked solid and permanent, could easily be broken down into movable components, and were often moved from park to park, and from city to city, as changes in business dictated. Today very few still operate on the sites where they were originally located.

In its rides, its lights, and its illusions, the turn-of-the-century amusement park gave glimpses of a future filled with technologies that park visitors could not in their wildest dreams imagine would someday become part of their everyday lives. To those from a rural background who migrated to the industrialized cities in the hope of finding a better living, the trolley parks offered a reminder, in the form of the merry-go-round with its horses and barnyard animals, of the farm life they had left behind.

The millions of immigrants from Europe whose golden dreams turned to grim reality in drab, overcrowded tenements were able to see a touch of their homelands in the splendid carousels carved by their fellow immigrants. They could listen to familiar tunes and caress the exquisite handcrafted carvings, easing for a nostalgic moment their homesick yearnings.

The vast stretch of sand known as Coney Island had its beginnings as a quiet seaside resort, a nearby retreat from the crowds and bustle of New York City. Toward the end of the 19th century, Coney Island began a metamorphosis into the gaudiest, most dazzling mecca ever to lure seekers of excitement and entertainment. One park after another was built along Coney Island's sun-bleached boardwalks and glittering sands. The opening of each new enterprise was marked by great fanfare and lavish spectacle. Competition spurred each new park builder to outdo those who had come before. Each vied to draw visitors from competing enterprises by becoming bigger, better, and more visually astounding—and by offering more thrilling rides.

Coney Island's enormous success inspired scaled-down imitations in every city and town across America. Parks named Coney Island, Luna Park, and White City could be found everywhere. The handful of companies building carousels found they had to expand their facilities to keep up with growing orders.

Oregon
·

Oaks Amusement Park, Portland: Herschell-Spillman, 1924, three-row menagerie

Pennsylvania
·

Dorney Park, Allentown: Dentzel, 1901, three-row menagerie (in storage, used for special occasions)

Kennywood Park, West Mifflin: Dentzel, c. 1926, four-row

Rhode Island
·

Crescent Park, Providence: Looff, c. 1895, four-row, ring machine

43

The armored horse Goliath was a favorite with riders, especially boys, on P.T.C. #15 at Expo '86 in Vancouver, British Columbia.

To compete with the rapid development of newer, more terrifying rides, the carousel blossomed into an exquisite jewel box of intricate design, splendidly carved and decorated. The use of electricity to drive the mechanism enabled the builders to design more massive carousels—which sometimes were more than 60 feet in diameter, with four or five, and occasionally even six, rows of horses to ride.

Electricity also inspired the bedecking of carousels with a multitude of dazzling lights that sparkled from every possible surface. Brightly painted horses leapt and plunged to the strains of popular tunes. Baroque rounding boards, beveled mirrors, and intricately carved chariots all added to the dazzling effect. The carousel was a vibrant spot of whirling color and sound in every

park, a focal point of glitter and motion that lured throngs and set a festive mood.

Gustav Dentzel introduced the first menagerie animal, a gothic lion carved by his father, Michael, to America. Some other carousel builders, Looff, for example, always offered a choice of menagerie animals as well as the traditional horses to ride. Competition increased the trend. Carvers gave their imaginations free rein to re-create in wood beloved household pets, familiar farmyard animals, ferocious wild beasts, and strange mythological creatures. The rider could choose a mount to match his or her favorite fantasy. Yet, despite the appealing and flamboyant appearance of the new menagerie figures, they never could dislodge the popularity of the horse. After a few years, most manufacturers bowed to riders' preferences and went back to building the all-horse carousel.

The glittering expositions so popular during the last half of the 19th century were mammoth showplaces at which a glorified view of the miracles of progress astounded throngs. They also gave further impetus to the amusement ride business. Visitors to every exposition could take a ride on a carousel. The first American world's fair, held in 1853 at New York City's newly constructed Crystal Palace, offered a crude bucket-seated merry-go-round among its amusement rides.

In 1893, at the Columbian Exposition in Chicago, visitors rode an improved merry-go-round and gaped in wonder at the largest ferris wheel ever built: a 250-foot, 2,160-passenger monster. In 1904, the St. Louis Exposition commemorated the 100th birthday of the Louisiana Purchase. The rare, four-abreast C. W. Parker merry-go-round that ran at that exposition was later moved to Portland, Oregon, where, according to more recent owners, it

Kennywood Park in West Mifflin, Pennsylvania, near Pittsburgh, and its prized jewel, a 1927 Dentzel carousel, were both named National Historic Landmarks in 1987. The four-abreast carousel's outside-row standers alternate between typical dignified Dentzel steeds and the more vigorous Muller carvings. Still in its original location, the carousel circles in a spacious, modern-looking, fifty-year-old domed pavilion. At the park you can also see a small kiddie carousel built by M. C. Illions.

When Colorado's Kit Carson County commissioners bought P.T.C. #6 from Elitch Gardens in Denver, the $1,250 price so outraged local citizens that the three commissioners lost any chance of reelection. Today's commissioners, along with the rest of the county, are devoted to the preservation of this rare work of art with its original paint. The commissioners even take their turns at the Auchy clutch.

became a popular attraction at Jantzen Beach Amusement Park. Today this carousel spins as the theme of the Jantzen Beach Mall, which replaced the park in the early 1970s. (There is some doubt that the carousel is actually that old, because its figures are in a style Parker was not yet building in 1904.)

The completion of the Panama Canal was celebrated in 1915 by the Panama-Pacific Exposition, for which a king-sized Dentzel carousel was moved to San Francisco from Balboa Park, San Diego, where it had been an attraction during the 1913 exposition. The 1912–1914 Herschell-Spillman carousel that circled in 1940 on the Gayway at the Golden Gate International Exposition on Treasure Island in San Francisco Bay now operates at Golden Gate Park, where it was refurbished by a seven-year, $888,000 restoration project that was completed in 1984.

Carousels continue to be part of every American world's fair and exposition. One of the finest wooden carousels ever made, the Philadelphia Toboggan Company's #15, attracted millions of riders at the Vancouver, British Columbia, Expo '86. That huge four-row machine, which carries only jumping horses, was completely restored and refurbished for the event. It was the only antique ride operating there, among a gaggle of wild, hi-tech rides.

Amusement park architecture was as rococo and overblown as the Victorian carpenter Gothic and cast-iron styles of the time. You can see striking similarities between the grinning jester head on a Dentzel carousel shield and a satyr or gargoyle leering from the cornice of a contemporary cast-iron building. You can find a regal 19th-century lion guarding a library or prowling a carousel. The serene face of a goddess may grace a building pilaster or a carousel's rounding board. Scenes from mythology, lavish festoons of leaves, fruit, and flowers, and other themes from classical Greece and Rome were common design elements embellishing both public buildings and amusement parks. They reflect an age when opulence and exuberance of design were considered aesthetic necessities of life—for those few who could afford them. Those with slimmer pocketbooks could enjoy them for a day. All they needed was a ticket to the end of the trolley line and a few nickels to pay for the amusement rides.

The Lochman carving machine, invented in 1903 and in widespread use in the industry within a decade, strongly influenced the carousel's style and future. With it, four animal bodies and heads could be roughed out simultaneously, using a finished piece as a pattern. Use of the carving machine did limit the variety of poses and styles possible, but because the finish work was still done by hand, each carver was free to put his

imprint on an animal's final appearance. Standardization never reached assembly-line precision; it only influenced the poses of horses produced in the final years of the Golden Age in the carving shops which made use of the machine.

The glorious era of the carousel and the amusement park sputtered to a stop like a damp firecracker with the Depression of the 1930s. The last wooden machine was built about 1930. Of the five thousand hand-carved carousels estimated to have been constructed during the preceding half-century, fewer than 200 survive today. Only about 150 of the old, all-wood, hand-carved carousels still operate. Many of those now in storage will never run again. The number of amusement parks has shrunk from a peak of about 1,500 in the 1920s to fewer than 200 major parks, including about two dozen large theme parks, in the 1980s. Fewer than sixty amusement parks and theme parks can offer rides on authentic wooden carousels.

The financial difficulties the country suffered in the thirties were not the only factor in the decline of the amusement park. Customers who had enthusiastically frequented the early trolley parks were now captivated by the novelty and freedom offered by the automobile. In its own car, a family could now explore the

Flowers bloom behind the saddle of the hippocampus on P.T.C. #6 in Burlington, Colorado.

47

Although the carousel was only rarely a part of the circus, clown parties have been a tradition at Portland's carousels to celebrate birthdays, anniversaries, and promotions on the job, and to entertain special groups. Gene Crommett, one of the wood-carvers who worked on the restoration of Portland's Looff carousel, rides Carol's Carousel.

countryside on a rapidly increasing number of roads. No longer were they limited to the destination of the streetcar tracks.

The growth of the motion-picture industry also affected the way in which people spent their leisure time. Sitting in a darkened theater watching the action on a screen appealed to some fun-seekers more than did going to an amusement park.

The Great Depression killed off the wooden carousel industry, but World War II sealed its coffin. When carousel manufacturers joined other industries in a giant conversion to wartime production, many skilled workers and tools were lost to the trade forever. A postwar era of economic controls effectively banned construction of such expensive "toys" as carousels. Companies sold out or closed down. Today none of the old companies still creates those magical wooden dream machines.

As manufacturing plants and warehouses spread from the cities out over the countryside, the area surrounding a park deteriorated, often spelling the park's doom. People were hesitant to venture into a rough district. Vandalism and declining revenues that made upkeep unaffordable caused further slumps in gate receipts. The less successful parks, caught in the crunch, closed down in great numbers during the 1930s and 1940s, victims of a changing economy and a shifting outlook on how to spend leisure time.

Many of the surviving parks occupy land that is a prime target for development for commercial or housing use. Crescent Park, in Riverside, near Providence, Rhode Island, closed finally in 1977, its land purchased for commercial development. A group of citizens formed "Save Our Carousel, Inc.," launching a powerful campaign to keep in its original location one of the finest carousels ever built. The spectacular machine was created in 1895 by the master carver Charles I. D. Looff, whose carousel factory was nearby. The carousel was designed to be an animated catalog of the variety of Looff's carvings. Its listing on the National Register of Historic Places acknowledges its historic value. For several years the preservation project seemed doomed in the face of "progress," but local feelings ran high, bolstered by support from local and state government officials and from carousel buffs across the country. Their persistence finally won out. Today the carousel, refurbished through a fund-raising campaign, is again filled with happy riders, proof of the power of public sentiment. It is the only amusement ride in a green oasis of park facing the water and conducive to family activities.

The fate of the carousel from Paragon Park, at Nantasket Beach in Hull, Massachusetts, was also threatened by progress. The popular park closed in 1984 after seventy-nine years of

operation. An ambitious commercial development was slated for the site, and P.T.C. #85, a favorite of generations of local residents and summer vacationers, was auctioned off. A group of devoted local supporters saved it and triumphantly moved it and its building (a 40-ton load) to a nearby site where it operates as "The Carousel Under the Clock."

The story of P.T.C. #12, the fabulous carousel from Crystal Beach, Ontario, across the river from Buffalo, New York, has no such happy ending. It was broken up in 1984. According to contemporary accounts, the park's owners explained that the carousel was sold to "keep the bank happy," and they stipulated that the auctioneer should accept bids only on the individual parts. Bidders at the carousel's auction had no chance to acquire the machine as a unit. Another piece of carousel history disappeared forever.

In 1989 the mixed carousel from Seattle's Fun Forest was broken up and the pieces sold at auction. Within a short time the owner announced plans for extensive improvements to Fun Forest, including the addition of a new fiberglass carousel. Carousel-lovers question the "improvement" at the cost of losing a fine example of the work of Carmel, Looff, Illions, Stein & Goldstein, and Allan Herschell that had been put together by carousel entre-

The Indian pony with a rose tucked under its ear seems right at home in the wide expanses of the eastern Colorado high plains country where P.T.C. #6 runs at the Kit Carson County Fairgrounds.

49

preneur M. D. Borelli. The carousel was a fine example of Borelli's penchant for covering all surfaces of carousel animals and chariots with far more jewels than the carver ever intended.

In 1970 the Chance Company of Wichita, Kansas, bought out the Allan Herschell Company of North Tonawanda, New York, the last of the old-time carousel makers. Chance still manufactures merry-go-rounds. Their horses, for many years combination creatures with wooden bodies and metal heads and legs, are now made of fiberglass. Until recently, most Chance merry-go-rounds were small and simple in design and decoration. During the 1970s the company constructed two huge, elaborate double-decked carousels carrying fiberglass replicas of some of the most famous carousel animals. The carousels were built to order as showpieces for the Great America theme parks in Santa Clara, California, and Gurnee, Illinois. A few years ago, Chance bought the finely detailed fiberglass molds of some of the best of the old carvings that were made by Bradley & Kaye, an amusement ride company in Long Beach, California. Now they are producing larger, more antique-looking merry-go-rounds with replicas of old wooden steeds and rounding boards. Several other companies make small merry-go-rounds today, but none carries wooden animals and none

P.T.C. #85 was a popular ride at Paragon Park, Nantasket Beach, Massachusetts, from 1928 to 1985. When the land was sold for development, a local group bid successfully for the carousel and moved it and its building in one gigantic load to a nearby spot on the beach. Renamed "The Carousel Under the Clock," it began running in its new home on July 1, 1986.

This three-abreast menagerie was broken up at auction in 1989 and replaced by a new fiberglass machine, even though it had been a flamboyant fixture at Seattle Center's Fun Forest ever since it arrived there for the 1960 World's Fair. The mix of figures by Carmel, Looff, Illions, Stein & Goldstein, and Allan Herschell was bedecked with a multitude of jewels by Borelli.

Tilden Park Carousel, Berkeley, California (right).

is likely to do so. The costs would be prohibitive and skilled labor is no longer available.

In recent years carousels have become attractions in shopping malls from Florida to Oregon, from California to Rhode Island. Some are antique wooden machines, rescued from destruction by mall owners who realize their drawing power. Others are recent, elaborate double-decker creations, many imported from Italy. While they offer satisfying dazzle and glitter, their fiberglass European-style ponies are small, plain, and unmuscular. They show only the most distant kinship to the finely carved wooden steeds that once pranced in circles all across turn-of-the-century America.

The old-time "carny" atmosphere has disappeared from many carousels. Their homes now are more often in city parks or commercial developments than amusement parks. The man or woman who operates the carousel today may be a law student, a retired engineer, a dentist, or a university professor devoting weekends to the low-paying job that years before had helped finance his or her way through college. Although the pay is low, there is enjoyment in sharing the delight of a ride on a colorful old-time machine.

This Herschell-Spillman prancing goat is aboard the Oaks Park merry-go-round, Portland, Oregon.

A dozen factories created the carousels that graced America's city parks and amusement parks or traveled with carnivals and fairs. While it lasted, it was a colorful world, peopled with colorful, talented men.

Dream Makers and Their Toys: The Carousel Builders

It never was a large industry. Yet for a time the carousel-building business enjoyed a booming success. About a dozen factories, centered in Brooklyn and North Tonawanda, New York, Philadelphia, Pennsylvania, and Leavenworth, Kansas, built the five thousand or so carousels that at one time whirled riders in horse-heaven circles throughout America.

Charles I. D. Looff—one of the greatest carvers, designers, and builders—moved his shop from Coney Island to Riverside, Rhode Island, and finally to Long Beach, California.

One company played "change-partners" to become in turn the Armitage-Herschell Company, the Herschell-Spillman Company, and the Allan Herschell Company (which had bought out the Spillman Engineering Corporation) before it was bought out in turn by the Chance Manufacturing Company in 1970. That company is now making lavish fiberglass carousels from molds of some of the fine historic animal figures.

Several factories sprang from the dreams of carvers building their first carousels piece by piece in their spare time. Financial success operating those first machines led to full-time work: establishing factories and hiring carpenters, carvers, painters, and other workers. The growing number of orders that came in were from parks and carnivals eager to have the most up-to-date model of the most popular amusement park ride. Gustav Dentzel and Charles I. D. Looff both did carving that set the styles other

carvers followed. Although in their later years they were involved more with the business end of the operation, they still unwrapped their chisels and worked in the carvers' shop, their first love, when they found time.

As orders for the newfangled machines poured in, the shops streamlined their work by developing a production-line system. Some workers glued boards together to form the hollow boxes that made up the bodies and the blocks from which legs and heads were carved. Others did the actual carving of the bodies and legs. Only the most skilled carvers were allowed to sculpt the heads and the ornate trappings of the outside-row animals. In most cases a single figure was the work of a group of craftsmen with varying degrees of skill. When the Lochman carving machine made it possible to rough out four body parts at one time, many companies turned to the carving machine, reserving the finishing work and decoration for their best carvers.

Some factories only built carousels. Others not only built but also operated them. Among the latter were Charles I. D. Looff, the Dentzels, and the Philadelphia Toboggan Company, which, in addition, produced other amusement rides and buildings to house their carousels. The C. W. Parker Company expanded their prod-

Owner T. M. Harton ordered elaborate trappings by carver Daniel Muller to be added to the outer-row animals, including this already fabulous dapple gray on his Dentzel carousel at Hunting Park in Philadelphia. The carousel was moved to Cedar Point in Sandusky, Ohio, in 1968 and is now known as the Kiddieland Carousel.

The Auchy clutch from P.T.C. #15 is an invention that produced a smoother ride and less wear on the carousel. It was developed by mechanics at the Philadelphia Toboggan Company, but the patent was issued to Henry Auchy, one of the company's founders.

uct line to supply just about everything needed to operate and transport a carnival.

E. Joy Morris, a Philadelphia designer and inventor of amusement rides, formed a company with his three brothers and began assembling carousels in 1896. In addition to building chutes (water slides) and coasters, he had a carvers' shop and built carousels for Chestnut Hill, Philadelphia (in 1892); Lakemont Park, Altoona, Pennsylvania; North Beach, Queens, New York; Vinewood Park, Topeka, Kansas; and possibly (in 1906) P.T.C. #6 for Elitch Gardens, Denver. These carousels were the first of about eighty carousels built by the Philadelphia Toboggan Company, founded by Chester E. Albright and Henry B. Auchy, under contract for whom Morris built some of their earliest carousels.

Although the Philadelphia Toboggan Company produced about eighty carousels in thirty years, by far its biggest business during all but a few of those years came from building roller coasters, which it continued to design and build long after it ceased carousel production in 1930. The company still stocks parts for its carousels and for the Auchy friction drive which became the standard mechanism for propelling their carousels, but its main business today is manufacturing Skee-Ball games.

In the early days the Philadelphia Toboggan Company found that it was sometimes easier and more profitable to lease rides than to sell them outright. As a result, they remained involved in amusement park operations throughout the life of their carousel-manufacturing business. They sold the last carousel they owned and operated to Cedar Point in the late 1960s.

Manufacturers such as the W. F. Mangels Company, Kramer's Karousel Works, M. D. Borelli, and T. M. Harton built carousel mechanisms. They never hired carvers, but bought all of their carvings from other shops, sometimes putting animals from several carvers on one machine, which complicates identification and establishing their history.

Among the most prolific of carousel producers were Parker, the Allan Herschell Company, and Norman & Evans of Lockport, New York. Because most of their machines were small carnival models that were set up, taken down, and moved dozens of times every season, their portable carousels wore out more rapidly than the more stable park machines. Therefore, few can be found today. In fact, no carousels from the Norman & Evans factory are known to be intact, although a steady stream of them poured from their plant during its existence.

A few small carousel companies operated in Ohio, mostly in the Cincinnati area, but only two possible Ohio-made carousels, from the U.S. Merry-Go-Round Company, are listed on the National Carousel Association's census or list of carousels. Nei-

The 1986 Junior Rose Festival princesses choosing a horse at Willamette Center, Portland, Oregon.

Bickleton, Washington, in the high desert country north of the Columbia River, has a Herschell-Spillman track carousel that runs once a year in early June during the community's annual Pioneer Picnic and Rodeo. This kind of carousel runs on tires on a circular track beneath the deck.

ther of those has been identified positively as having been built by that manufacturer. One of the "possibles" (which may be a C. W. F. Dare) operates two weekends a year at the U.S. National Cathedral in Washington, D.C. The other runs in Albion Boro Park, Albion, Pennsylvania.

The Identity Problem
■

The absolute identification of the carver of a carousel animal or its factory is often impossible. You may hear carousel buffs and collectors arguing the matter vociferously, but surefire identification is hard to come by, except for the rare animal that is stamped underneath with its carver's name. Only a few display a name, a monogram, or a portrait carved into the design of their trappings.

There are many reasons for the confusion. To begin with, at the time the horses and other carvings were being created, no one in the industry could imagine that provenance would ever matter. They were putting together machines to be sold and operated for financial gain. The animals and other carvings were designed to attract customers, to tempt them into spending a nickel for a ride. No one thought of them as works of art future collectors would pay astronomical prices for and throngs of carousel buffs would travel great distances to admire and ride.

When factories closed or changed hands, their stock of animals, chariots, and other parts was usually bought up by another company and used as replacements or to fill out machines. Their carvers were hired by other companies, taking their characteristic styles with them to be adapted to their new employer's expectations. Detailed records of who did what were seldom kept, even by the Philadelphia Toboggan Company, which, because one employee took it upon himself to start the system, numbered its carousels. The numbering system is a boon to historians, as it allows the travels of P.T.C. carousels to be traced more accurately than any others.

Carvers moved from factory to factory, depending on which builder was in a period of high production. Some carvers opened their own factories, where they carved for the machines they produced and did contract work for other factories. For example, the Muller brothers—Daniel and Alfred—worked as young men for the Dentzel factory, where it is thought that Daniel designed the models other Dentzel carvers followed. They probably next moved for a short time to the Philadelphia Toboggan Company, taking their unique carving styles with them. Then they went into business for themselves, as Daniel C. Muller and Bro. During the time their shop was in operation, from about 1903 until 1917, they built carousels, with mechanisms built by T. M. Harton or others, that they sold or operated themselves. They also did contract work for Dentzel, P.T.C., Long, and probably for others.

They eventually went back to work for the Dentzel factory during the last years of its operation. They worked there and at P.T.C. with other top carvers, notably Salvatore Cernigliaro and Frank Carretta. It is impossible to imagine that these men did not get inspiration and ideas from each others' work.

Work on P.T.C. #15 was begun in 1906, but the order for the five-row #17, which the company rushed to complete for Chicago's Riverview Park, took precedence. With the exception of the outside row of standers on #17, the horses, rounding boards, and chariots created for the two machines were similar almost to the point of duplication. In fact, the numbers stamped on the horses show that some of #15's outside-row horses fit into the middle of the sequence for #17, indicating they were probably built at the same time.

A Muller horse owned by Duane and Carol Perron has a ram's head behind the saddle.

A very three-dimensional, elaborate collar is worn by a horse aboard Carol's Carousel, owned by Duane and Carol Perron, in Portland, Oregon.

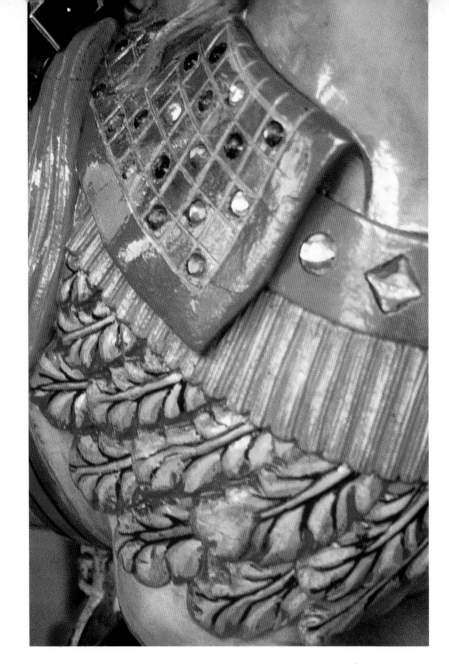

A cohesiveness of style is apparent in the almost floating feeling of #15's horses, yet you can see on one horse the slight sneer, distinctive Roman nose, and lack of a forelock that identifies a Stein & Goldstein horse. A number of small, inside-row topknotted ponies and huge, elegant outside-row jumpers show the easy-to-spot characteristics of Muller animals. In the rush to finish, P.T.C. must have called on the S&G and Muller shops for help.

Example could be piled upon example to show why the subject of identification is clouded by confusion. For that reason it is best to enjoy the animals for their beauty, while familiarizing yourself with carvers' and builders' styles. Indulge in educated speculation, but don't worry unduly about the animals' pedigrees. Listen to the expert guesses of those who have been close to the carousel world, but remember that no one's word is final.

Chipping Away at History: The Carvers and Their Carvings

A handful of master carvers from Europe worked magic with their chisels to produce strong, handsome carousel figures. In America their work took on new vigor and creativity. Their carvings made the carousel come alive. The best of their work transcends craftsmanship to become an art that recalls happy memories of a bygone era.

From glued-up slabs of wood, a small group of master carvers chiseled the magnificent steeds that we remember from childhood rides on the carousel. The carvers were driven by the need to fill pending orders for carousels. They were simply building utilitarian objects designed to last only as long as they remained useful. Except for a few carvers who were also builders and who occasionally put name, initials, or, even more rarely, a self-portrait on a favored animal, they didn't sign their carvings. Their lives were lived in obscurity, their histories unrecorded.

What motivated them? Was carving a carousel animal more fun than carving a piece of furniture? Was it more lucrative? Or was the work simply more available? We cannot know. But from studying the flowing, vigorous lines of the best of the breed, it becomes clear that the animals were truly the product of inspiration, and that the carvers shaped into each figure a bit of themselves.

As so often happens with artists, recognition was late in arriving. But, while the last of the great carvers was still alive, awareness of the quality and lasting artistic value of their work had begun to grow. Salvatore Cernigliaro was a master carver for the Dentzel factory. His skilled hands were responsible for the lively charm of many of the favorite menagerie animals on Dentzel carousels. In 1974, shortly before his death, the National Carousel Association made the ninety-four-year-old "Cerni" an honorable member. He was presented with his membership certificate by the president of the National Carousel Association.

The cats Salvatore Cernigliaro carved hold birds or fish. You can ride this alert feline at Knott's Berry Farm in Buena Park, California.

This typical sign is on a center panel of the Herschell-Spillman Greenfield Village Carousel at the Henry Ford Museum in Dearborn, Michigan. It has horses, a variety of menagerie animals, and four chariots, including a spinning tub and a rocking chariot.

Some of the earliest carousel carvers in this country were farmers who turned their skills to something lucrative during the slack winter months. Others were shipwrights in search of a new career, for wooden sailing ships were being replaced by ships with iron hulls, which didn't need carved figureheads and sternboards. Most carvers were cabinetmakers and furniture builders who saw in that growing new field the opportunity to make good use of their talents in ornamentation. Few had had backgrounds in carousel making in Europe before they emigrated. Only two, John Zalar and Daniel Muller, had any formal training in sculpture and art.

Carvers frequently moved from one shop to another as work volume changed or as they were offered more money. They took their distinctive carving styles with them, and eventually influenced, and were influenced by, the new shop. So it is often impossible to identify positively the work of a single carver.

An example of names lost to history is that of the carver who created the appealing dog who seems to be chasing a butterfly on the West Endicott Park carousel in Union, Broome County, New York. A similar one frolics on the Highland Avenue Park carousel, also in Union. Both carousels are from the Allan Herschell Company. Roy and Allan Herschell, grandsons of the company's founder, when shown a photograph of one of the dogs, said they were not aware that such carvings existed. Possibly an itinerant carver had come through North Tonawanda and stayed long enough to carve these dogs and the pelt saddles portraying lions and wolves that can be found on these carousels.

The Carvers and Builders and Their Work

■

Charles Carmel b. 1865, Russia; d. 1932

In 1883, at age eighteen, Charles Carmel brought his seventeen-year-old bride, Hannah, to the United States from their native Russia. Details of his life have not been recorded, but he is thought to have carved carousel animals from about 1900 until 1920. He worked for Charles I. D. Looff in Brooklyn until Looff

As far as owners Duane and Carol Perron can tell, this Looff tiger is unique. Looff carved his other tigers in the style of the Spokane prowling tiger.

■

This lifelike dog romps on the West Endicott Park Allan Herschell carousel in Union, New York. The only other dog like this is aboard another carousel in Broome County, New York. The identity of the talented carver is a mystery.

moved his business to Rhode Island. He then set up his own carving shop in Brooklyn, near Coney Island, from which he sold to the carousel builders in the area.

Carmel carved very few menagerie animals. His dramatic horses exude strength and action, yet their expressions are always gentle. He liked to carve horses with heads tossed back or vigorously arched. Many had tongues that lolled out. He used either wooden or horsehair tails, and carved wooden horseshoes on his steeds, in addition to lush, decorative trappings. His armored horses are especially impressive and vigorous.

Charles W. F. Dare b. ?; d. 1901

Almost nothing is known of Charles W. F. Dare and the Brooklyn-based New York Carousal (sic) Manufacturing Company he founded. One of the early carousel makers, Dare was building small, primitive carousels as early as 1866. He continued to build carousels until his death in 1901, after which the company closed. He produced winsome menagerie animals and small, perky horses. He also supplied the trade with other amusement devices.

A lack of concrete information makes it difficult to identify with any certainty the carousels of Dare and the other early companies. Only a handful of primitive machines have survived. The small, c. 1890, two-row Washington Cathedral carousel was attributed to Dare by *Carrousel Art* magazine. The NCA census lists it as a 1913 product of the U.S. Merry-Go-Round Company. The Watch Hill Flying Horses in Rhode Island and the Martha's Vineyard Flying Horses are two different styles of carousels that have been identified as carved by Dare.

Gustav A. Dentzel b. c. 1846, Kreuznach, Germany; d. 1909; and William H. Dentzel b. c. 1876, Philadelphia, Pennsylvania; d. 1928

Gustav Dentzel was one of the few carvers and builders who had a family background in carousels. In Kreuznach, Germany, Gustav's father, wheelwright Michael Dentzel, built his first carousel in the late 1830s. Michael's carousels were popular with customers and financially successful.

In 1864, when Gustav was eighteen, he sailed for the New World. In Philadelphia he set up his business as a cabinetmaker, and was traveling with his first portable carousel before 1867. On

Knoebels Amusement Resort in Elysburg, Pennsylvania, has one of only four pure Carmel carousels you can find operating today. Carmel's horses have flowing manes, naturalistic heads, and gentle expressions.

Carol's Carousel in Portland, Oregon, has a mix of Illions and Carmel horses. This outside-row Illions is typical of that carver's work. Note the undershot jaw, wide nostrils, forward-staring eyes, and forward-swept mane.

Gustav Dentzel migrated to the United States in 1864. He was originally a furniture builder, but after his first carousel was a great success, he changed his occupation to carousel builder. This center panel sign hangs in the home of his grandson, William H. Dentzel II, in Santa Barbara, California.

Charles Dare built primitive carousels, only two of which are known to have survived. This one, The Flying Horses of Martha's Vineyard, runs at Oak Bluffs, Massachusetts. The horses have sulfide marble eyes, with tiny images of animals or other figures embedded in them.

this primitive machine he used some figures he had brought with him from Germany. After it proved a financial success, he went into the carousel-building business full time, moving his shop to the Germantown section of Philadelphia. His earliest machines were human propelled, then horse powered. In the early days, Dentzel, like many other pioneer carousel makers, operated some of his own carousels. He built America's first amusement-park-style carousel in 1867 and operated it at Smith's Island in the Delaware River just off Market Street in Philadelphia. This was the first two-abreast hores-propelled carousel and the first operated at a permanent site.

When steam, and later electricity, became practical, Dentzel was the first to use them as motive power for his ever-larger, more elegant, more elaborate machines. He soon found the demand for park carousels so great he expanded his business. He employed his sons, William (Billy) and Edward (Eddie), and other members of his family in his busy factory.

After Gustav's death in 1909, his son William took over the business. Some of the finest carvers worked at one time or another for the Dentzel Company, among them the Muller brothers and Salvatore Cernigliaro. After William H. Dentzel's death in 1928, the factory closed. Some carvings were donated to the American

Museum of Public Recreation, founded in 1929 by William F. Mangels. The remainder of the equipment and carvings was sold to the nearby Philadelphia Toboggan Company, whose use of Dentzel figures on P.T.C. carousels further confuses the problem of identification.

Dentzel horses, especially the outside-row standers, were carved in a limited number of classic stances. Even the jumpers seldom show vigorous motion. The company used the same poses repeatedly, which simplifies their identification. Ornamentation and trappings were restrained, although they became less so when William H. Dentzel took over the factory. However, the Dentzel factory did not use jewels. Natural hair was used for tails on early horses, but practicality eventually called for a change to carved

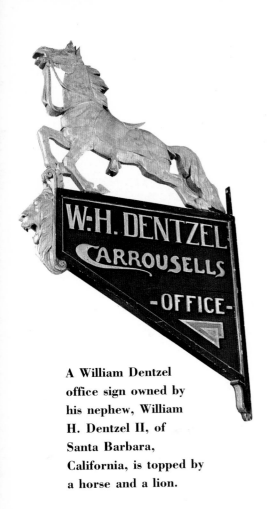

A William Dentzel office sign owned by his nephew, William H. Dentzel II, of Santa Barbara, California, is topped by a horse and a lion.

A two-abreast Armitage-Herschell carousel from Coeur d'Alene, Idaho, is now owned by Carol and Duane Perron.

■

wooden tails. Dentzel saddles are short and flat with a low pommel and curved cantle. Like Looff and others, the Dentzel factory made some bird saddle backs.

The Dentzel factory's use of lifelike colors for the animal bodies resulted in formal-appearing, sedate carousels. Dentzel menagerie and exotic animals are popular, especially the lifelike cats, rabbits, dancing bears, and other species created by the talented artist Salvatore Cernigliaro, who designed and carved for the Dentzels for a quarter of a century.

The Dentzel factory built mostly park machines, which were so substantial and well constructed that many are still running today.

Allan Herschell b. 1851, Scotland; d. 1927

Allan Herschell's contribution to the world of the carousel was significant. He formed more companies, built more carousels, and was in the business more years than any other builder. Three years after coming to America from his native Scotland (in 1870), Herschell became a partner in a factory that built steam engines and boilers in North Tonawanda, New York, near Buffalo. In 1883, despite protests from his partners, Herschell built his first "steam riding gallery," an early merry-go-round. It was a hit. He built another in 1894 and a third in 1895 that ran at the World Exposition in New Orleans. By 1891 his partners were won over and became believers in the newfangled rides. They shipped steam merry-go-rounds at the rate of one per day, or 100 per year, depending on which historian you believe.

In 1903 Herschell and his brother-in-law, Edward Spillman, formed the Herschell-Spillman Company, which became the world's largest maker of carousels. Their small, portable machines were designed to travel with carnivals. Their large, more elaborate ones became the magnet that drew customers to many parks, mostly in the East and Midwest. They did, however, deliver some across the country, and two went as far as Tahiti, where their steam boilers were fired not with wood but with coconuts.

Fine examples of large Herschell-Spillman menagerie park carousels can be found at Balboa Park, San Diego; San Francisco's Golden Gate Park; Tilden Park, Oakland, California; Oaks Park, Portland, Oregon; Greenfield Village, Dearborn, Michigan; and Trimpers Rides, Ocean City, Maryland. Poor health forced Herschell to retire in 1911, but by 1915 he was back, forming the Allan Herschell Company. After his final retirement in 1923, that company remained in business. It bought out Spillman Engineering in 1945 and sold out finally to the Chance Manufacturing Company in 1970.

In the 1980s the original Allan Herschell factory building in North Tonawanda, New York, was turned into a carousel museum, with an operating Allan Herschell carousel. Herschell produced probably the largest number of portable carnival-style carousels during his long career on his own and in partnership with Armitage and Spillman.

Kennywood Park, West Mifflin, Pennsylvania, and its Dentzel carousel are registered as National Historic Landmarks. This outside-row stander (preceding page) shows the upstanding topknot, wild eye, and vigorous stance typical of Daniel Muller's carving. On the outside row these dashing horses alternate with the gentler Dentzel horses.

The small merry-go-rounds turned out in the final years of the Allan Herschell Company were far from the elaborate, baroque icons produced by Looff, Dentzel, and P.T.C. They were small, portable machines with distinctively out-of-proportion figures that traveled on innumerable carnival circuits. Steeds from later Allan Herschell machines were imitated in aluminum and then fiberglass. They can be found today in traveling carnivals across the country. Chance still builds simple metal and fiberglass portable machines. In the 1970s they created two massive double-decker wedding cake "Columbia" carousels for the Great America parks in Gurnee, Illinois, and Santa Clara, California. Dave Bradley, owner of Bradley & Kaye of Long Beach, California, had made molds of fine historical carvings to cast in fiberglass. In the mid-1980s Chance bought the molds. Since then Chance has been producing carousels for parks that want the nostalgic look of an old carousel.

Marcus Charles Illions b. 1871, Russia; d. 1949

Marcus Charles Illions learned the carving trade in his native Russia, then in Germany, and then in England from Frederick Savage. He came to Brooklyn in 1888 in the employ of the animal-showman Frank Bostock, who imported Savage amusement rides. Illions worked for Looff and later with carousel-maker William F. Mangels, for whom he carved figures and other wooden decorative parts.

In 1909, Illions founded the M. C. Illions and Sons, Carousell (sic) Works, and employed members of his family in the business of creating entire carousels. An authoritarian and a perfectionist, Illions allegedly insisted on carving every animal head himself. Most of his carousels stayed at Coney Island. He carved ornamentation for roller coaster cars for scenic railway builder Lamarcus A. Thompson and created Luna Park's opulent Roman-chariot ticket booths. Other carvers considered Illions' work to be the finest.

Illions' style was exaggerated, flamboyant, and animated; it glowed with color and jewels. He created wildly upswept and forward-swept manes, carved flat and textureless so they could be covered with gold leaf. His trappings were lavish and flowing. His horses are distinctive for their small, undershot jaws and high-set, forward-staring eyes. Illions had not far to look for models for his steeds. He owned a stable and rode every morning. For relaxation he created intricate sand sculptures on the beach near his Coney Island shop.

The Long Family (Built carousels 1876–1903)

The phrase "Long-Mixture" appears in several places in the National Carousel Association census. Although the name Long is not usually listed on the roll of carousel makers, the family did build eight carousels between 1876 and 1903, and they have been in the carousel business one way or another ever since, longer than any other family.

Brothers Edward F. and Fielding Long brought their families from England in 1858 to settle in Germantown, Philadelphia. More than a century ago, Uriah Long carefully carved a miniature crank-operated merry-go-round as a Christmas gift for the children in the family. Someone suggested that perhaps building a full-sized merry-go-round might be fun and profitable. That was the start of the family's involvement, which continues today. The family's descendants are connected with several amusement parks.

The Longs built the frames and did the decorative work. They hired out the mechanism construction to the Lusse family, whose descendants now build the Lusse Auto Skooter, an amusement park ride. The horses for the first machine were carved by Charles

Frogs with flying coattail saddles are among the unusual figures you can find on Herschell-Spillman menagerie carousels. This dapper one is on the Greenfield Village Carousel in Dearborn, Michigan.

Recreation Park in Binghamton, New York, is in the process of restoring its large, four-abreast carousel. This jumper is a typical Allan Herschell horse, with its almond-shaped eyes and enlarged head tucked low.

This rare Dentzel kangaroo, the only one on an operating carousel, is at Watkins Regional Park in Largo, Maryland. Its hind legs are hinged so it carries riders on leaps high into the air. The carousel operated at Chesapeake Beach, Maryland, from 1929 until 1972.

F. Leopold, Sr., who worked as boss carver for the Dentzel, E. Joy Morris, and P.T.C. carving shops.

In 1876 the Longs set up their first crude machine in Fairmount Park, Philadelphia. It was a two-abreast machine propelled by a horse. After operating there for a time, it was sold, and its whereabouts faded into oblivion. That is, unless it is the machine that found its way to Watch Hill, Rhode Island. There is speculation that Watch Hill's "Flying Horses" may be that first Long carousel. The Longs built their first three-abreast menagerie in 1892. Before selling it, they operated it for three years at Ontario Beach, near Rochester, New York. The family slept and cooked in one half of a tent set up near the carousel; the other half of the tent housed the noisy, smoky, kerosene-fueled steam power plant.

For Edward F. Long's daughter, Lois, and her husband, John Outhwaite, the family built a machine that rotated clockwise. The Outhwaites installed it as the first ride in the amusement area at Blackpool Beach in England. Another carousel was built in 1899 for George W. Long, Sr., who installed it at Sea Breeze in Rochester, New York, in 1904. It ran there until 1925, when it was exchanged for George Long, Jr's, P.T.C. #36, then at Seneca Park. It ran at Seneca Park until the winter of 1942, when some thoughtless ice skaters built a warming fire on its wooden deck. The ensuing blaze completely destroyed both the carousel and its building.

The last of the Long carousels was built in 1903 and has always stayed in the family. A three-abreast menagerie, its animals were carved by master carver Daniel Muller and his brother, Alfred. Thomas V. Long, grandson of Edward F. Long, bought the

New Philadelphia, Ohio, has a large city park, Tuscora Park, created and developed by strong community effort. Its well-cared-for carousel, a Herschell-Spillman, now gallops in a new, protective building. The three rows of horses show Herschell-Spillman's diverse styles.

This richly caparisoned Illions armored horse is aboard the Wyandot Lake Park Carousel in Columbus, Ohio.

Carousel carvers only rarely carved their names onto the animals. M. C. Illions carved into the trappings of this fine horse not only "Designed and carved by M. C. Illions," but an excellent self-portrait. The carving is owned by Rol and Jo Summit of Flying Horses in Rolling Hills, California.

■

This P.T.C. #36 stander at Sea Breeze in Irondequoit, Rochester, New York, was recently restored to its original colors by Susan Hofsass, granddaughter of the original owner, George Long.

machine from the family in 1908 for $3,500. After operating it at several sites, he moved it to Bushkill Park, outside Easton, Pennsylvania, which he'd bought in 1934. In addition to operating the park, Long was active in buying, selling, restoring, and operating carousels. He carved several of the figures now on that carousel, to replace damaged Muller animals. After his death in 1965 his widow, Mabel (whom he had met when she was riding one of his carousels), kept the family-style park running until her death in 1989. The carousel still has a ring machine and two band organs that provide musical accompaniment. Another popular Bushkill ride is the "Over-the-Jumps" built by Tom Long. It resembles a one-row carousel, but the animals and spinning tubs are fastened to the revolving deck, which rolls on an undulating track to give a jolting ride as it circles.

Over the years members of the family have owned a number of carousels built by other manufacturers and operated them in parks all across Pennsylvania and New York State. Sea Breeze, on Lake Ontario, at Rochester, New York, is now being run by members of the fifth and sixth generations of Longs in America.

Charles I. D. Looff b. 1852, Schleswig-Holstein, Denmark; d. 1918

Charles I. D. Looff's genius shone both as a carver and as a carousel builder. The initials I. D. sprang, according to folklore, from the question of an immigration authority as to his middle initial, which was needed for I. D. "All right," replied Looff. "It's I. D."

As one of the early carvers, and one of the most successful, his style exerted a strong influence on other carvers.

Looff imparted some of his personality to his beloved wooden animals. They reflect his gentle outlook, warm humor, love of animals, and pride in his adopted land. His genius at carving shows in the multiplicity of animal personalities he created during his long career. In addition to horses, he carved a wide variety of menagerie animals. His earliest ponies and menagerie creatures were simple, lovable, and sweet-faced. He progressed to vigorous—but always happy—steeds that reflect his knowledge of anatomy and his feel for texture and for history. Finally, his mounts became the epitome of speed and stylization. He never carved an animal with a mean expression. And he never resorted to the assembly-line production of the carving machine.

Looff showed a never-failing eye for the flamboyant, which collectors have classified as "Coney Island Style." It was his strong belief that the animals, the carousel, and the building that housed them should be inseparable parts of a dynamic whole, a kaleidoscope of light, color, sound, and action. One of the finest results of this belief is the carousel and building he built at Crescent Park, Rhode Island, near his factory. This imaginative machine was designed as a catalog-in-motion of his work. After years of being threatened with destruction it is once again spinning riders into worlds of fantasy. You can still circle to the sound of the Ruth und Sohn band organ while squares of colored glass in the building's clerestory windows paint the carousel with a multicolored kaleidoscope of light.

Daniel Carl Muller b. 1872, Germany; d. 1952; and Alfred F. Muller Born 18??, Germany; d. 19??

Daniel Carl Muller (the name is correctly pronounced Mewler, but most carousel enthusiasts say Muhler) was the son of Dentzel carver Henry Muller, who had brought his family to America from Germany in 1881. The brothers showed extraordinary carving skills when as youths they worked for Gustav Dentzel. Daniel studied sculpture with the famed Charles Grafly at the Pennsylvania Academy of Fine Arts in Philadelphia, even

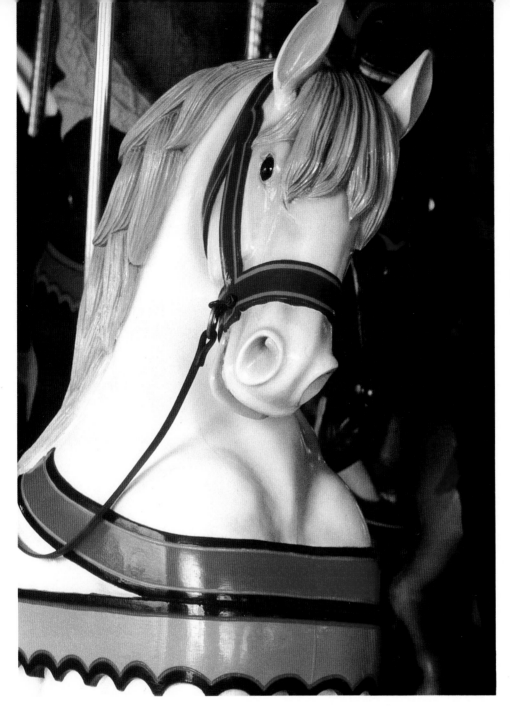

while heading his own carousel factory and carving shop. His
sculpture won top awards in art competitions.

From 1903 to 1917, under the name D. C. Muller & Bro., the
two brothers combined their carvings with T. M. Harton mechanisms. They produced a number of fine carousels, some of which
they operated themselves.

Their designs and carvings can be found on many carousels
other than their own, as they often worked on orders for other
carousel-makers. World War I brought material shortages and
other problems to the industry, making it necessary to close their
shop. Eventually, they went back to work for William Dentzel until
the latter's death in 1928.

"Popcorn" is a late-style Looff horse photographed on the Portland Looff Carousel when it was running at the Willamette Center in downtown Portland. It shows the fluid motion and the super-reality of Looff's late period. The lolling tongue is more characteristic of Carmel's work than of Looff's.

Daniel Muller's carving style is characterized by unequaled strength, realism, and a feeling of motion. A serious student of the Civil War, he often lavished accurate detail of military trappings on his outside-row horses. The delicacy and detail of his carved flowers and ribbons are unsurpassed. Alfred Muller, Daniel's younger brother, worked with Daniel all of his life, but he stood in the shadow of his more gregarious older brother's carving genius. Little has been recorded about him, and it is not known how much of the work attributed to "Muller" is actually Alfred's.

Charles Wallace Parker b. 1864, Griggsville, Illinois; d. 1934

Charles Wallace Parker was the most flamboyant showman in the colorful world of carousel-makers. With characteristic modesty, he crowned himself "America's Amusement King" and gave himself the title "Colonel" for good measure. He founded and reigned over the Parker Amusement Company, the "World's largest manufacturer of Amusement Devices."

Parker was one of the few native-born Americans in the carousel-manufacturing business. In 1892 he became part owner of a secondhand merry-go-round. He immediately saw ways to improve carousels through innovative design and construction. He branched out into owning traveling carnivals. Eventually his factories could supply almost any carnival need, from band organs to tents, from concession stands to portable power units—even the railroad cars that hauled the components from fairground to fairground.

Among Parker's employees were "carnies" who traveled his carnival circuit during the summer season. When he moved his operations to Leavenworth, Kansas, in 1911, he used cheap convict labor from the nearby penitentiary. World War I prisoners of war are also said to have been in his employ.

Most of his "carry-us-alls" were small and portable, designed for use in traveling carnivals and fairs. His catalogs were peppered with testimonials from satisfied buyers about the superior earning power of his machines and the ease and speed with which they could be erected and dismantled—an advantage in beating the competition for customers' coins.

Fewer than two dozen of Parker's hundreds of portable carousels have survived the rough life of carnivals constantly on the move. Despite Parker's glowing advertisements of the quality of his products, his animals were not sturdily constructed—glue without dowels was a shortcut but was less substantial. Most broke or wore out fast, victims of long seasons of hard use.

Most Parker merry-go-rounds stayed in the Midwest. His closest competition came from the Herschell factory in North Tonawanda, New York. The Theel Company of Leavenworth,

The "T. M. H. Co." monogram on this horse carved by Daniel Muller signifies the T. M. Harton Company, which bought horses from other companies and assembled them on Harton frames.
The owners are Rol and Jo Summit of Flying Horses in Rolling Hills, California.

The carousel at Jantzen Beach in Portland, Oregon, has typical stretched-out Parker horses. This photograph was taken in 1968, just before the park closed down to make way for the Jantzen Beach Center. The carousel is one of only four park machines built by C. W. Parker, who concentrated on small, portable merry-go-rounds.

Kansas, bought out the Parker Company after Colonel Parker's death. Theel still uses aluminum horses taken from molds made from hand-carved wooden Parker steeds.

Unlike most of the builders, Parker was not himself a carver, but he had a strong influence on the styles of the company's horses. During the first few years, his machines carried sweet-faced horses not very different from early Looffs and Dentzels. Then his carvers devised a characteristic Parker horse, the most easily recognizable of any breed, designed for easier stacking and moving. The Parker horse is unique in appearance: in violent motion, with legs stretched almost horizontally, nostrils flaring, head held down and sideways or flung high with mane wildly tossing, eyes bulging. Parker made no pretense of copying life. He wanted to produce a feeling of fantasy and speed. He succeeded.

Parker's colorful, stylized horses, bedecked with colored jewels and mirrors, display widely diverse trappings. An ear of corn behind many of his saddles saluted Kansas. Patriotic trappings included flags, emblems, shields, and eagles. Fish, dogs' heads, and other animals appear behind other saddles. Flowers cascade from the necks of some of his more flamboyant steeds. The horses' bodies and trappings were painted every color on the painter's palette without regard for realism.

Philadelphia Toboggan Company (P.T.C.) Built carousels c. 1903–c. 1931

The Philadelphia Toboggan Company factory was located in Germantown, a suburb of Philadelphia, Pennsylvania. ("Toboggan" in the name alludes to the early coaster rides made by the company.) The company was founded in 1903 by two successful young businessmen, Henry Auchy and Chester Albright. Neither man was a woodcarver, but at one time or another P.T.C. had on their payroll most of the best carousel carvers. E. Joy Morris built some of the early P.T.C. carousels. The Muller brothers probably worked for P.T.C. briefly before going into business for themselves, and did carving for P.T.C. while operating their own carving shop; Frank Carretta was the company's carving foreman for many years; and Charles Carmel worked for P.T.C. Leo Zoller carved large horses and chariots for P.T.C. from 1907 to 1911. Auchy offered a job to Salvatore Cernigliaro, but his loyalty to Gustav Dentzel kept him at the Dentzel factory until it went out of business. After that, he did go to work for P.T.C. Because P.T.C., like other companies, ordered carvings from free-lance carvers to fill in when they were busy, their carousels often carry the work of many carvers.

During the thirty years the company was in operation it produced some of the finest of American carousels. P.T.C. was the only company that numbered its machines throughout its history. Its records have enabled historians and carousel buffs to trace the migrations of P.T.C. machines more completely than for any other company.

P.T.C. #72 at Kiddieland in Melrose Park, Illinois, is a fine, beautifully maintained example of the later work of the Philadelphia Toboggan Company. You can find P.T.C. monograms on several of the shield horses. The scenery panels have original paint.

This early P.T.C. sea dragon was on the carousel at Quassy Amusement Park in Middlebury, Connecticut. It was stolen in the mid-1980s and eventually replaced with a modern carving that is an excellent match for the original. The carousel was broken up at auction in 1989.

The Albion Boro Park Carousel in Albion, Pennsylvania, was built by the U.S. Merry-Go-Round Company. The two-abreast carousel was restored in 1987 and 1988 by volunteers and proudly rededicated during a visit in 1988 by National Carousel Association conventioneers. The carousel was formerly horse-propelled. Restorers discovered that one section of the old deck lifted to let the horse into the center of the carousel.

Stein & Goldstein
Solomon Stein, b. 1882, Russia; d. 1937; and
Harry Goldstein, b. 1869, Russia; d. 1945

Both Solomon Stein and Harry Goldstein came to America from Eastern Europe and settled in Brooklyn, New York. While carving carousel horses for the W. F. Mangels Company, they decided to open their own Brooklyn factory. They did, in 1912, in partnership with Henry Dorber, who built the carousel mechanisms. Two years later Dorber left to operate one of the company's carousels, and Stein and Goldstein reorganized as the Artistic Caroussel (sic) Manufacturing Company. They carved the horses' heads and hired other carvers to complete the figures. The business operated until 1918, during which time they built only about a dozen complete carousels. Subsequently, the two carvers worked for other companies.

Stein and Goldstein built some of the largest carousels ever. Their five- and six-abreast machines carried up to one hundred riders, but proved to be unwieldy, hard to power, and slow to load and unload. None of the giants have survived. A vigorous four-row

S&G with huge horses is a popular attraction in Central Park in New York City. An elegant three-row machine graces Bushnell Park in Hartford, Connecticut, within view of the state capitol. A charming two-row model designed for youngsters runs in a wooded glen at Knoebels Amusement Resort in Elysburg, Pennsylvania, which also has a large, four-row Kramer-Carmel carousel.

Despite the short time they were in business, Stein and Goldstein left an impressive mark on the carousel-carving craft. An entire carousel of Stein & Goldstein steeds is a sight to fill the viewer with awe: a triumph of power and motion, of wood transformed into dynamic action.

Other Carvers

■

Frank Carretta, Salvatore Cernigliaro, Leo Zoller, and John Zalar stand out among the little-known carvers who worked miracles turning wood into horseflesh. So little was recorded about them in their time that their lives remain pretty much mysteries to us, yet their work is remembered and appreciated by all carousel lovers.

P.T.C. #62, at Santa Monica Pier in California, has been the scene of action in many movies, most notably *The Sting*. The horses are large and ornately decorated, like this one with its tiger-pelt saddle blanket.

Only four Stein & Goldstein carousels are still in operation. The one at Bushnell Park in Hartford, Connecticut, has large steeds with characteristic Roman nose, no forelock, flattened-back ears, wild eyes, and slight curling of the lip that make the work of these carvers popular with men but often intimidating to children.

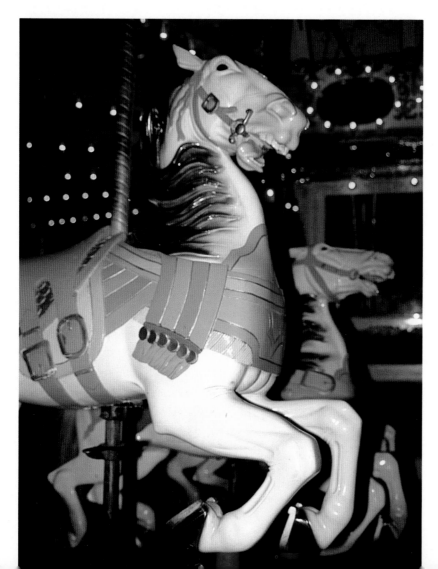

■

Los Angeles' Griffith Park has since 1937 been home for a mixed carousel being restored by its owners, Warren Deasy and Rosemary West, while it is in operation. This armored Spillman Engineering horse joins Looff and Carmel steeds on board.

Master carver Frank Carretta worked for the Philadelphia Toboggan Company from about 1912 until the company closed in the 1940s. Salvatore Cernigliaro, like Carretta, came from Italy as a young man. He worked loyally for Gustav Dentzel, creating dashing horses and the most beloved menagerie animals, especially cats, rabbits, and small, winsome dancing bears. After the Dentzel factory closed, he worked for P.T.C.; he spent his final years teaching art. His carousel horse sketches show that he was as highly skilled with a pencil as with a chisel.

For many years John Zalar was given credit for the fine early work at P.T.C. until someone thought to ask his son when Zalar began carving carousel animals. He said it wasn't until long after the early animals had been done. We can only surmise that his name was confused with that of Leo Zoller, P.T.C.'s first master carver. This information was brought to light through the detective work of Barbara Williams, Barbara Charles, and Charles Jacques, Jr. If so, Zoller left his mark on the early P.T.C. styles (from 1907 to about 1911) and Zalar on the late ones: different styles, but both impressive.

William F. Mangels, T. M. Harton, Fred Dolle, E. Joy Morris, Timothy (?) Murphy, George Kramer, Henry Dorber, and M. D. Borelli are the names of most of the men who built carousel mechanisms—the iron and steel that made the carousels spin. They are only vaguely familiar to the carousel lover.

The only carousel frame builder whose name is well known today is William F. Mangels. He built mechanisms for which Illions, Carmel, Looff, and others furnished the horses. But he is known, too, for inventing the Razzle-Dazzle (1891), the Tickler (1906), the Whip (1915), and other rides; for his patented improvement of the Savage galloping mechanism (1901); for building small kiddie merry-go-rounds, many of which are still delighting small riders; for creating in 1929 the American Museum of Public Recreation (which closed in 1955); and for writing the bible of the industry, *The Outdoor Amusement Industry: From the Earliest Times to the Present*. The book, published in 1952 and long out of print, is full of astute observations on that segment of Americana, and preserves some of the industry's history for future generations.

T. M. Harton (the "M" is for Marshall) built frames for carousels carved by the Muller brothers. He was also the founder of Pittsburgh's West View Park, a designer of roller coasters and fun houses, and an operator of carousels in several amusement parks.

E. Joy Morris designed and patented a "toboggan slide" and became involved with carousel building in Philadelphia just before the turn of the century. His shop built carousels and supplied carved figures for other carousel manufacturers.

The questions we have about the similarities and anachronisms in the work of carousel carvers will probably never be explained. It may have to be privilege enough for us to look upon and to ride the products of their fertile imaginations and their artistic skills.

At Six Flags Great Adventure in Jackson, New Jersey, you can ride one of only two English roundabouts operating in the United States. This large, elaborately decorated portable machine runs counterclockwise. It was built by Savage of Kings Lynn and ordered by carnival operator Patrice Williams, whose name is proclaimed on the rounding boards, a custom in Great Britain.

■

This stander with a helmeted face shield hung in front of the saddle was destroyed along with the rest of P.T.C. #38 in a tragic fire at Dorney Park in Allentown, Pennsylvania, in 1983.

Carousels and Parks, Here and Gone

The thousands of turn-of-the-century amusement parks and city parks each had its carousel—small and simple or gaudily ornate. Only about 150 of the old wooden machines remain in operation today. The rest have disappeared, victims of fire, flood, greed, or neglect.

Each of the old carousels and parks has its own story of happy times and sad. There are too many stories to tell in one book, so a sampling will have to do.

Because George F. Johnson had to go to work at age thirteen in a shoe factory in his native Upstate New York, riding a carousel whenever he wanted to was a dream denied him. That is why Broome County, New York, now has more merry-go-rounds per capita than anywhere else. In time Johnson built an empire of shoe factories, and he and his family donated six Allan Herschell carousels to Binghamton, New York, and to the surrounding towns where his employees lived. So other children wouldn't be deprived of rides, the cost of a ride has always remained the one Johnson set: a piece of litter.

Yes, Broome County is the *county* where you may ride the most carousels. The *city?* Portland, Oregon, has three carousels operating year-round, several kiddie carousels, and at least two more full-sized ones that spin during the warmer months—plus another dozen in storage awaiting locations for operation. The *park* where you can ride the most? Cedar Point on Lake Erie in Sandusky, Ohio. Three million visitors a year have their choice of five historic carousels at Cedar Point, including a racing derby 90 feet in diameter.

Dorney Park near Allentown, Pennsylvania, shares its natural tree-shaded setting with free-roaming wild deer that can be

Carol's Carousel, Portland, Oregon.

seen from the park's roller coasters. It has been run as a traditional park for more than a hundred years. But today you can't ride on a classic wooden carousel there. The park's beautiful 1903 Dentzel menagerie comes out of storage only for special occasions. The full-time carousel is a new fiberglass one. The story of Dorney Park's carousels recalls sad memories. The Chanticleer, a rare European rooster and ostrich merry-go-round used as a set for the 1968 Rosalind Russell movie *Where Angels Go*, was destroyed by fire in 1973. "Le Grande Carrousel," P.T.C. #38, an exquisitely maintained three-row 1916 machine had operated at Dorney for fifty years when it too was wiped out by fire in the fall of 1983. Of the two carousels, all that remain are the wooden ostrich snatched from both fires—and many memories.

Residents of Spokane, Washington, are prone to rhapsodize proudly about their beloved carousel. The story behind it is a romantic one, but may be partly fairy tale. One of the most ornate carousels ever carved by Charles Looff, it was supposedly created as a wedding present for his daughter, Emma. What is certain is that she and her husband, Louis Vogel, operated it in Spokane's Natatorium Park. They operated it so successfully, they were able to buy the park, which remained in the Looff family until 1952. When, in 1968, the park closed forever, the carousel was put into storage, and there was some talk of selling it. But it was too deeply woven into the childhood memories of the people of Spokane for that. Funds were raised to purchase and restore it. Bill Oliver, the

P.T.C. #6, Kit Carson County, Colorado.

Rides atop this large Allan Herschell elephant at Waldameer Park in Erie, Pennsylvania, are only memories now. The mixed carousel was broken up at auction in December 1988.

Jantzen Beach, a large amusement park built on the Columbia River in Portland, Oregon, by the company that makes Jantzen swimsuits, was open from 1928 until 1968. A rare Parker four-abreast park carousel operated in this gazebo in the park.

last operator of Natatorium Park, who had first ridden the carousel when he was two years old, took charge of the restoration work, which began in 1972. The carousel was installed in the heart of the city, in Riverfront Park, on the banks of the Spokane River. The opening celebration on May 8, 1975, was a festive one, the fulfillment of the dreams of an entire city. Bill Oliver, his mission in life complete, died at the carousel a week after the dedication ceremonies.

In 1982, in Kit Carson County, Colorado, shortly after the restoration and rededication of P.T.C. #6 was completed, four of its rare animals (with their original paint) were stolen. The county's residents were numb from shock, and carousel lovers from all over felt they had lost a piece of history. Six months later, the animals were found, undamaged, in a warehouse piled with stolen antiques. When the animals were brought home, a spontaneous parade formed to welcome them back. Those beloved animals had been residents of that remote eastern Colorado ranching community for more than half a century.

The Watch Hill Flying Horses is a two-row Dare, dated by the National Carousel Association to about 1884, but it is possibly much older. The twenty small steeds, each carved from a single log, have horsehair manes and tails and sport real leather saddles and ears. The horses are suspended by chains fore and aft and are spun outward by centrifugal force as the machine speeds up. The origin of the Flying Horses is not certain, but the story handed down for a century is that it was left behind at Watch Hill when a traveling carnival disbanded. It was originally powered by a live horse who, according to the merry-go-round's historian Harriet C. Moore, during the winter missed his work and the children. He would escape from his stable whenever he could and find his way to Watch Hill to tread the circular path around the carousel.

In Kiddieland, at Knoebels Amusement Resorts near Elysburg, Pennsylvania, is a two-abreast machine at the far end of the scale from the usual huge Stein & Goldstein horses. It is a 1915 portable carousel with twenty-eight junior-sized S&G horses and two chariots. Lawrence Knoebel had years ago operated it on the fair and carnival circuit. It was sold in the 1950s, but in 1975 the delighted family located and repurchased it and installed it in an honored spot in their popular and picturesque park.

Stories abound of rescue and restoration by townspeople and civic groups all across the country. Each story is one of efforts to catch hold of the childhood dream and keep a beloved carousel for future generations to enjoy. The list of locally owned, nonprofit carousel operations includes almost half of the still-intact wooden carousels that are either in operation or are expected to be put into operation in the near future. The groups operating these carousels include branches of government—from towns and cities (about forty) to national (one, at Glen Echo Park, is under the National Park Service but is managed by a foundation)—a church (the Washington Cathedral), and nonprofit corporations or commissions.

You can find carousels run by local support groups at fairgrounds, firemen's parks, historic villages, zoos, museums, and at city parks. It is these carousels that are most safe from being broken up for collections. Their owners are people whose families have ridden them for generations and who themselves have ridden them throughout their lives. They are determined that future generations will have the same privilege. People who work to keep these carousels running say that they are as much a part of the family, town, or city as their own children. Many amusement park owners feel the same way, but as economic threats grow, owners face difficult decisions.

The Broadway Flying Horses in San Diego, California, was built about 1895 and probably operated first at Coney Island. Moved to Salisbury Beach, Massachusetts, the Mangels frame was outfitted with Looff figures: an outer row of standing horses, goats, and dogs and two inner rows of jumping horses. It opened in 1980, housed in this building at Seaport Village; a larger carousel building is planned to handle the crowds.

An armored horse on the rare all-Carmel carousel at Rye Playland in Rye, New York. Only four all-Carmel carousels are still in operation.

■

Jantzen Beach Amusement Park in Portland, Oregon, was razed to make room for a vast complex of shopping center, offices, apartments, condos, and yacht and houseboat moorages. The carousel, the only remaining part of the park, is the popular hub of the Jantzen Beach Center. It has been the scene of several marathons, the last of which broke all records with a 325-hour ride, with the riders spending 50 minutes of every hour on the spinning merry-go-round.

Carol's Carousel, Portland, Oregon.

The 1926 four-abreast Spillman Engineering/Looff/Carmel carousel in Los Angeles' Griffith Park (far left) first operated at Mission Beach in San Diego. It was on view at the San Diego Exposition in 1934 and 1935 and has been at Griffith Park since 1937. The carousel often appears as a setting for scenes of motion pictures.

Historical Crossroads Village, near Flint, Michigan, is reached by riding the steam train from the distant parking lot depot. In addition to a turn-of-the-century Main Street, a picturesque farmstead, and other buildings from a rural past, it has a 1912 Parker carousel, restored and operated by local residents. The unusual jumping horses are propelled from underneath.

Idlewild Park, northeast of Pittsburgh in Ligonier, Pennsylvania, is a charming complex in a woodsy setting, popular for group picnics. The park is especially proud of P.T.C. #83, a beautifully restored three-abreast carousel with many fine horses—several with P.T.C. shields. It came to Idlewild in 1931 from Atlantic City, New Jersey.

This brown outer-row horse is aboard P.T.C. #85, the Carousel Under the Clock in Hull, Massachusetts. The carousel formerly ran at nearby Paragon Park.

Carol's Carousel, Portland, Oregon.

■

Wyandot Lake Park, part of the Columbus, Ohio, zoo, has one of the very few pure Illions carousels still in existence. This carousel, on its Mangels frame, originally ran at Olentangy Park in Columbus. Slots in the deck allow the horses to fly outward as the ride speeds up.

■

The San Francisco Zoo carousel, a colorful Dentzel/Illions menagerie, is a very popular ride that runs just inside the zoo grounds. It has vivid red sweeps and some fine Cernigliaro carvings, including these charming flirting rabbits.

The Shoreline Village 1906 four-abreast Looff carousel (far below left) on the waterfront in Long Beach, California, has some delightful carvings, especially its rows of four leaping goats, camels, and giraffes. Before coming here in 1982, it ran at Luna Park in Seattle, Washington, and at Playland-at-the-Beach in San Francisco.

P.T.C. #47, an elaborate four-abreast model built in 1919, is the centerpiece of Hersheypark's Carousel Circle (left). It has been beautifully restored and, like the rest of the theme park in Hershey, Pennsylvania, is kept in immaculate condition. It came to Hersheypark in 1949 from Liberty Heights Park in Baltimore, Maryland.

■

The same technologies that produced the Jacquard loom, the Swiss music box, the pipe organ, and the musical clock were used to create the band organ. It seems as if the carousel is propelled not by steam or electricity, but by the nostalgic tunes from the old band organ.

Music, Music, Music

Imagine spinning silently on a carousel. Oh, there is the occasional creak of old wood, a whisper from the well-greased gears, the plaintive sigh of the breeze stirred up by the revolving machine. It is a haunting feeling you get gliding enveloped in that ghostly near-silence. Something vital is missing.

To be complete, a ride on a carousel needs a sprightly tune from the splendid baroque band organ. It needs the music as much as it needs the painted wooden steeds and the gentle gliding up and down motion as it spins in circles. It was discovered early in the carousel's history that music was a crucial ingredient to spice up the carousel ride, when the first enterprising itinerant musician cranked his simple hand-held barrel organ to accompany the movement of the circling horses.

Although barrel organs used at the carousel became larger and more complex, their design limited them to a few tunes, all of the same length, which was determined by the diameter of the cylinder, or barrel, whose pins produced the music. Only so many pins will fit on a cylinder, as only so many bars of music will fit on a page.

Band organs and the earlier barrel organs belong to a large and varied group of automatic—or mechanical—musical instruments. They range from those rare Swiss pocket watches that contain musical movements to a few automatically played carillons. In Europe, as early as the 16th century, wood- or metal-

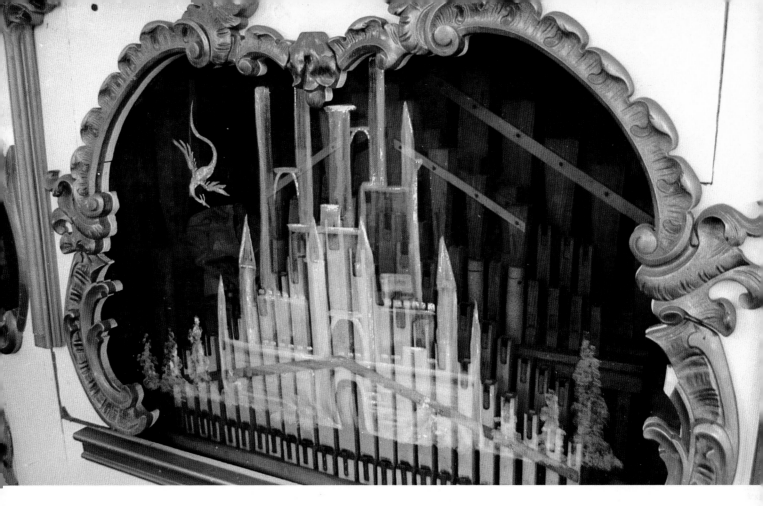

barreled instruments in which metal pins activated the vibrating members produced music. The cost of those early, handmade automatic instruments made them available only to the very wealthy.

The pinned-cylinder barrel organ provided music for the carousel until 1892, when the organ builder Ludovic Gavioli developed the first book organ in Paris. He had been inspired by the 1805 invention by Joseph Marie Jacquard of a perforated book that automated the pattern-weaving loom. With the new system, tunes were played from folded books—accordion-pleated stacks of pierced cardboard fed automatically through the band organ. The open holes activated the organ pipes. The folded book allowed tunes of varied length and tonal quality to be played.

When steam power became practical to drive the carousel, an auxiliary steam engine was added to crank the organ's bellows and feed the music. As electricity came into use on the carousel, it was also applied to power the band organ's bellows and music-feeding system.

Emile Welte, of M. Welte und Sohn of Freiburg, Germany, patented in 1889 his invention of a pneumatic action system for using punched paper rolls (similar to piano rolls), which made it possible to extend greatly the length of play.

The invention of a system of double tracker bars made it

Chiappa band organ owned by Duane and Carol Perron.

Carousel historian
Frederick Fried
demonstrates a small
Molinari barrel organ,
also called a hurdy-
gurdy, from his
extensive collection
of carousel memorabilia.

This small steam engine
was once used to power
a band organ. It is on
display at Ferrymead
Museum in Christchurch,
New Zealand.

possible to play one roll while rewinding another. That eliminated a waiting period of silence that was broken only by the flap-flap of the roll being rewound.

Band organs became larger and more highly decorated, and the playing mechanisms became more intricate. They could reproduce the sounds of many instruments and give the effect of a complete marching band or concert orchestra. On some models the drums. cymbals, trumpets, and other instruments were visible to the riders. The most elaborate band organs had animated figures of music conductors and musicians. All these improvements combined to ensure the band organ's becoming a symbol of the joy of riding a carousel.

For many years after the carousel became popular, all band organs were imported from Europe. Eugene DeKleist, a German, founded the North Tonawanda Musical Barrel Organ Factory and began building band organs near Buffalo, New York. He sold out to Rudolph Wurlitzer in 1908. Other factories built in the North Tonawanda area were Artizan, the North Tonawanda Musical Instrument Works, and the Niagara Instrument Company.

To keep producing their music, band organs need expert servicing and tuning annually. Unfortunately, over the years many band organs were not kept up as they should have been, and because they no longer played well they were eventually discarded. They have been replaced by recorded band organ selections—and sometimes even popular or rock music, which is inappropriate. No other music can satisfy the true carousel or band-organ lover—or evoke the bewitching nostalgia of the band organ.

In one small factory near Bellefontaine, in rural Ohio's farming country, new band organs are being constructed by the same techniques used in the old factories. Don Stinson had been in the business of repairing band organs, until, in 1975, he saw the need for new ones and decided to try building them. He recruited and trained his neighbors in the exacting craftsmanship necessary to construct a high-quality instrument. The demand for his fine instruments has expanded tremendously, and today they enhance the ride on many carousels.

Only one company is currently producing band-organ rolls commercially. Play-Rite Music Rolls, Inc., of Turlock, California, founded in 1960, has applied computer technology to the process developed a century ago. The company has designed equipment that reproduces copies from old rolls.

It is encouraging that craftsmen are again building band organs—and music rolls for those band organs to play—thus carrying on the tradition of joining music to the carousel ride.

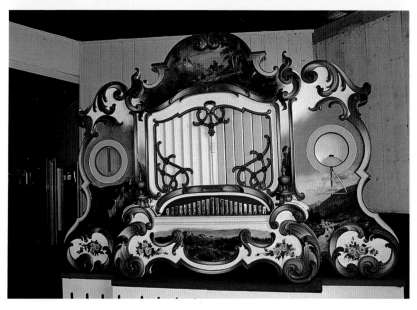

These folded books are used with a Dutch street organ at Dutch Village in Holland, Michigan.

The double trackers on this Wurlitzer 146-B allow one music roll to play while the other is rewinding.

The Wurlitzer Monster Military Band Organ at P.T.C. #6 in Burlington, Colorado, has only one volume—loud—but the tone is impressive. Drum, trumpets, and pipes can be viewed from inside the center housing or through the many-paned windows.

This Wurlitzer 165 band organ was purchased new in 1926 to accompany P.T.C. #36 when that carousel was moved by George Long from Seneca Park to its present location at Sea Breeze in Rochester, New York.

The Calliope Is Not a Band Organ

The circus calliope, raucous and happy sounding, is a very different instrument from the carousel's band organ. Early calliopes were powered by steam, rather than by an air bellows. The music is usually made by a musician playing on a keyboard, although some calliopes are mechanized. The sound is produced by steam whistling through metal (or less often, wooden) pipes; the sound is shrill, loud, and designed to carry a long distance. It is as piercing as the whistle on a steam locomotive or a steamship. The calliope was intentionally designed to be loud—to call townspeople from afar to come to the circus parade or to announce the arrival of a Mississippi riverboat. The sound is too loud and too harsh for a carousel, which needs the compatibility of a band organ's more mellow, complex notes.

This Gavioli fairground organ was in badly damaged pieces before Harvey Roehl rescued and restored it.

Saving Pieces of Our Past: Collecting

As the number of carousels has dwindled, the number of collectors has multiplied. The result is fierce competition for rare pieces that has caused prices to sky-rocket. Too many carousels that should still be running have been demolished to feed the demand by collectors. One alternative is to collect carousel memorabilia.

The days are long past when you could hope to make a lucky find of an abandoned carousel—or even a single carousel animal—in some forgotten barn or attic. Today, if you want to purchase an example of even the simplest of the hand-carved remnants from America's past to adorn your home or office, you would almost need to take out a mortgage to do so.

Most of the major carousel collectors across the country started collecting when carousels were less scarce and less endangered, and while prices were low. As collectors became more sophisticated about what they wanted, they bid prices up, tempting many carousel owners to sell at auction. In addition, the auction houses have a regrettable practice of adding 20 percent to the total of the individual bids to arrive at the minimum bid for the complete carousel. Thus, buyers who want to keep a carousel intact must pay a hefty penalty.

Too many fine pieces have by now found their way into museums or private collections, and few of the rare ones are even for sale. Not enough pieces are placed where they can be seen by the public.

Dealers and auctioneers who want a carousel consigned to their sales use the ploy that a carousel is expensive to insure and invites vandalism. Collectors often justify the dismantling of carousels by saying that the animals are works of art that will wear out on an operating machine. However, we have seen that carvings

An early P.T.C., probably built by E. Joy Morris, shows a parrot and draperies behind a saddle. This carousel was broken up at auction in 1989.

Knoebels Resorts at Elysburg, Pennsylvania, in addition to its large Illions carousel, has this unusual Stein & Goldstein carousel (far right). It is much smaller than the ones S&G usually created. The two-row portable was operated as a carnival ride for many years by the father of the present owners of Knoebels. It was sold in the 1940s, discovered and repurchased in 1975, and returned to run in the park.

P.T.C. #75 at Wonderland Pier in Ocean City, New Jersey.

kept in good repair and protected by paint look as good as new after a century of use. Some have even outlasted their mechanisms, which have had to be replaced.

The number of carvers working at the craft today is growing to meet an ever-increasing demand. Modern carousel animals lack the patina of age and the dignity of having lived through a century of imaginative history, but today's carver must charge nearly what an antique figure might cost because of the time he must spend carving one.

If you are in the market for a carving, you should be aware that old animals are being faked. Mexican pieces that are crude, of inferior craftsmanship, and smaller than the ones they are roughly copied from are being offered to unwary buyers. As prices escalate, wholesale imitation of the old figures is bound to increase. It pays to do your homework, to know what you are looking for, and to enlist the help of a reputable expert before you buy any figure.

Good quality fiberglass replicas that show all the detail of an ancient wooden steed are much less expensive and are gaining in popularity. The advantage of these sturdy animals is that molds can be made from the rarest and most desirable figures, making it possible to own a copy of a truly fine specimen. Painted, they cannot be told from the real thing without close, expert inspection. The fiberglass mold reproduces even the dowel marks, flaws, and seams of the original. And fiberglass figures don't contribute to destroying complete, operating carousels.

After considering cost, availability, and the fact that having an antique figure in your living room may be depriving thousands of riders of the pleasure of a spin on it, you may decide that your desires can be satisfied elsewhere. Collecting carousel memorabil-

A winged cherub is carved in full relief on the lovers' chariot on P.T.C. #15, shown before restoration.

ia is a less expensive hobby and can be just as much fun. Tickets, posters, postcards, signs, handbills, photographs, brass rings, and other items from the heyday of the carousel are still available if you poke around in secondhand shops and go to auctions. Persistence can pay off in a collection that exudes the feel of the old carousel.

With the rapidly increasing popularity of the carousel theme, many new items can be found that bear merrry-go-round designs: miniature carousel animals, coffee mugs, plates, jewelry, music boxes, greeting cards, wrapping paper, jewel-like pressed-glass cup plates and sun catchers, postcards, posters, patches, tee-shirts, jackets, sweatshirts, potholders, tiles, and jigsaw puzzles. Best of all, by collecting them, you will feel the thrill of collecting without contributing to the demise of the carousel.

The block of four carousel stamps issued in 1988 by the United States Postal Service was the most popular stamp of that year. It offers a challenge to collectors: How can you best display the stamps or the first-day covers with originality and color? Should you combine them with other collectibles or display them alone? The range of possibilities is endless. Certainly adding foreign stamps and first-day covers that also have a merry-go-round theme can enhance your array.

Artists and carvers have discovered the charm of the carousel and its carvings. Paintings, miniature sculptured figures, and entire miniature carousels are being created in growing numbers. Limited-edition prints of contemporary art depicting the carousel are popular not only with carousel buffs but with collectors of fine art prints.

Decorators have discovered in the merry-go-round a cheerful, nostalgia-evoking theme full of color, action, and grace of design.

The Steuben Glass Company of Corning, New York, has created exquisite cut-glass *objets d'art* with a carousel theme. One signed piece 7½ inches high revolves on its base to show nine glass panels on which stallions prance, leap, and gallop. Steuben created another merry-go-round piece, a bowl; a duplicate of it is on display in their museum. The original was presented as a gift by President Truman to Queen Elizabeth of England.

Finely carved miniatures in wood, pewter, or porcelain, often produced in limited editions, offer the discerning collector a chance to accumulate a menagerie that does not take up the amount of space full-sized animals demand. They can be a delight to examine, for they catch the essence of the original animals from which they are replicated. For example, the Floyd L. Moreland Carousel in Seaside Heights, New Jersey, offers a series of sculptures, each edition of which is limited to 250 pieces. The first miniature of the series is a horse, an outside-row Dentzel stander.

It is named "Dr. Floyd," for the professor of classics who operates the carousel. Such finely detailed miniatures as these, in such a small edition, and produced from an original sculpted by a fine artist, will surely become sought-after collectors' items.

A market has developed for complete operating carousels in miniature; some are very small, but others have a diameter of three feet or more. Some are accurate to the last minute detail, while others are the delicious manifestation of the artist's happy fantasies. These miniatures may be built of wood, blown and stained glass, pewter, silver, or porcelain enhanced with gold leaf. Some can be had for a few hundred dollars. Others are priced in excess of ten thousand dollars.

An original carousel figure is beyond the financial reach of most of us, and that is just as well. They are better kept on an operating carousel. But the variety of collectibles is unlimited and offers the best possible enjoyment of carousel collecting.

The carousel at Griffith Park, Los Angeles, California, has Spillman Engineering horses, as well as Looff and Carmel.

Restoration of a carousel involves painstaking work: stripping off thick accumulations of paint; doweling, carving, patching, and regluing; replacing lost jewels; repainting; and overhauling the mechanism.

Elbow Grease and Glue: Restoration

Carousels that run every day, carrying thousands of riders on circular odysseys, need constant attention to keep them in good operating order. But eventually even the best-cared-for carousel must undergo restoration of its mechanism and animals.

The load on the bearings, which may be 20 tons on a large carousel, puts an enormous strain on the mechanism. Waves of riders climbing on and off the animals chip the paint and wear it thin. Legs, ears, and other vulnerable figure parts become broken and must be replaced.

Restoration may be done on a continuing basis, by removing one animal at a time and repainting it, and by shutting down, usually in winter or during a slack season, to go over and repair the inevitable wear to the mechanism. Some carousels close down completely to strip the machine down and go over each part.

Many carousels received a new coat of paint every year, building up layers of enamel that after enough years can reach a thickness of one-eighth inch. That much paint obscures the fine detail in the design. Stripping can reveal delightful surprises.

Cleaning, stripping, and repainting should not be done without consulting an expert. Old varnish, for example, can turn the paint on an animal so dark that its true colors can no longer even be imagined. Sometimes it is possible to discover the original factory colors. The original color may bond tightly to the primer and resist the stripping that will remove the less resistant layers. If

the original colors are there, a careful restorer will describe, sketch, and photograph them. If it is practical, he or she will duplicate them for repainting. Of course, the optimum method is to reveal the original paint and protect it with varnish.

Scenery panels and rounding boards are subject to less wear than the animals, so you will find original paint on more of them. They are, however, often dark with age and dirt. In the 1950s it became popular to paint over the old panels with cartoon figures. To regain the old look of the carousel, these coats of paint should be removed and the old paintings refurbished. This can be done if a coat of protective varnish was put over the original panels, so the later layers of paint can be removed without touching the original.

Each carousel has its own set of problems, so no one way of restoring will work for every machine. Restorations at amusement parks may be done in-house or by a professional restorer or restoration shop. Because that may be too expensive for the carousels owned by municipalities or local organizations formed to save the carousel, and grants and fund-raising drives may not bring in the tens or hundreds of thousands of dollars necessary, volunteers may be recruited to do some or all of the work. With the value of a carousel as high as it is now, this should only be done

This armored stander is pictured on P.T.C. #61 when it ran at Idora Park in Youngstown, Ohio. That park closed in 1984. The carousel, purchased at auction by David and Jane Walentas, is being restored for a Brooklyn, New York, waterfront project.

■

Knotted tails appear on several of the horses on P.T.C. #15, owned and restored by the Perrons.

with a sure understanding of the restoration process. If the work is not done correctly, it can have an effect on the carousel's value. The National Carousel Association is prepared to help by giving advice or referring you to experts.

All across America, groups are rescuing their local carousels and putting them back into operation. One restoration, that of the Kit Carson County, Colorado, carousel, P.T.C. #6, was made famous by being featured on the *National Geographic* television special *Treasures From the Past*, first aired in April 1987. P.T.C. #6 is a rare and elegant example of the finest factory paint. It was carefully restored by artist and conservator Will Morton VIII of Lakewood, Colorado, to bring back the brilliance and unusually intricate detail obscured by many years of wear and by darkening varnish. Art Reblitz of Colorado Springs, Colorado, restored the carousel's magnificent Wurlitzer 155 Monster Military Band Organ to its intended thundering clarity.

In Brooklyn, New York, members of the Prospect Park Alliance are trying to recapture the magic of the Prospect Park Carousel. The carousel, whose features include fifty-one magnificent horses, a lion, a giraffe, a goat, and two chariots, dates back to the early 1900s and is largely the work of noted carver Charles

This dynamic Muller horse was so thickly coated with years of park paint that there was no hint of the delicate detail of the lion and serpent on it. The horse is owned by the Perrons.

A horse on P.T.C. #36 (above left), at Sea Breeze in Rochester, New York, shows, behind the saddle, the head of a man with a pipe and wearing a cap.

Carmel. One of only twelve remaining Carmel designs, the carousel was brought to Prospect Park in 1952, from Coney Island, exactly twenty years after the park's first carousel was destroyed by fire. Renovated in the early 1970s, the present carousel was closed in 1983 because the gears and motor were no longer operable. The work to revive the original warmth and glow of the carousel's colors is being done by master sculptor and art conservator Will Morton VIII. The carousel figures will be restored to the style of color and detail orignally used and missing legs and ears will also be recarved.

Other restorations have brought back carousels that were in much worse shape. The four rows of jumping horses of P.T.C. #15, for example, after operating for years in parks in New York State, Ohio, and Wisconsin, had been stripped of their original paint by a dipping process that left the wood as dry as driftwood. Every inch of the lifeless wood was covered with hairline checks and large cracks. Laminations had curled and pulled apart. Chemical residues attracted and retained dampness, which prevented paint from adhering. The original colors were unrecorded.

When Duane and Carol Perron of Portland, Oregon, bought P.T.C. #15 in 1981, they knew they faced a painstaking restoration to bring the severely damaged animals back to life. Diane Vaught of Burlington, North Carolina, shared information she had discovered while heading up the project to restore that city's carousel which had suffered from a similar problem. Although P.T.C. #15 was the only antique ride at Expo '86 in Vancouver, British Columbia, it was so beautifully restored that many carousel watchers at Expo said it reminded them of the old carousels but it looked so good it must be a new fiberglass machine.

Restorations can cause more damage than good if the layers of paint are stripped without saving the original colors for the historical record and for protection. Careful stripping to the origi-

Flag horse on the Jantzen Beach merry-go-round, Portland, Oregon.

Ontario Beach is a large lakefront county park in Rochester, New York. Its Dentzel menagerie carousel is being restored and has a new Stinson band organ. The decorative panels are original.

nal finish coat, recording the colors, and then coating that paint with protective varnish before repainting will protect the original colors and help to preserve the wood, which is just as important. If the budget is tight and the carousel is to get heavy use, it is sometimes impractical to do a painstaking restoration back to factory appearance, but at least that first paint should be left on the carving and it and the wood beneath protected.

Two fine Dentzel carousels—both three-row menageries—the 1921 model at Glen Echo, Maryland, and the 1905 carousel at Ontario Beach, Rochester, New York, have had their animals' beauty obscured by many coats of ugly paint. Because both have the original paint beneath, it was recommended that each be restored as closely as possible to its original appearance. The paint on the scenery panels on both carousels is original and can be brightened by cleaning. The same is true of the only two-row Dentzel still in existence, the Highland Park carousel at Meridian, Mississippi, whose top-row scenery panels were done by the master artist and carver Salvatore Cernigliaro.

Working with old paint is hazardous, because the paint was lead based. The lead has permeated the wood and cannot be removed, so that sanding the bare wood puts lead dust into the air and your lungs. The chemicals used in stripping can also be dangerous. Only by knowing how to work safely with these hazards can you accomplish a good restoration without damaging your health.

A good restoration is a slow and costly process, and careful consideration is necessary to weigh the costs, the availability of a skilled restorer to do the work or give advice, the wear to which the carousel will be subjected by riders, and the significantly higher value of the machine if its integrity is maintained. Bringing a time-worn and damaged carousel back to its original beauty and usefulness can be a rewarding project. If done right, the carousel's life will be prolonged and it will continue to give pleasure to all who ride it.

A Look at One Restoration

■

How do you go about restoring a carousel that is in pieces, with some parts missing? It takes time, money, patience, space in which to work, artistic skill, mechanical deftness, and more patience and more money and more time.

There wasn't nearly enough money to hire a restorer to do the work needed on the fine Looff carousel Duane and Carol Perron own. No grant or institution would back the project. No one locally had experience in that kind of work. And when the project began in 1980, there were few experts in the field anywhere.

Still, the Perrons were determined to fulfill their dream of restoring and operating a unique carousel, one that would be a showcase of Charles I. D. Looff's carving, a rotating museum of the evolution of Looff's work—horses and menagerie animals—from about 1880 to 1914, from his earliest sweet-faced carvings to his middle-period realistic style, and to his last stylistic figures.

The Perrons' plea for volunteers brought an eager response. Each worker chose an animal to restore and spent at least one evening a week for the next two years on learning by doing. They named their animals. As they worked, some felt that their steeds came alive—that they spoke to them of their years on the carousel.

As layers of ancient paint—often either unappealingly gaudy or depressingly dull—came off, hidden details of carving appeared. Moments of excitement highlighted the hours of hard work. One worker discovered that the thick crust of paint on her early horse hid solid brass rosettes, rather than the plaster ones commonly found on Looff animals. When buffed, those jewel-like ornaments gleamed like 22-carat gold.

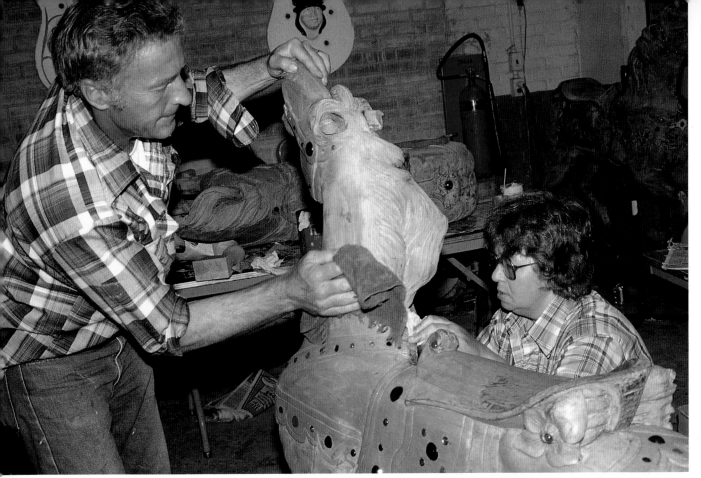

To neutralize the
stripping chemicals,
restorers Delma
and Gary Sprauer
wipe down the
horse they are
working on.

Carol Perron fills and
sands a P.T.C. flower-
bedecked outside-row
jumper she has named
"F.T.D."

■
114

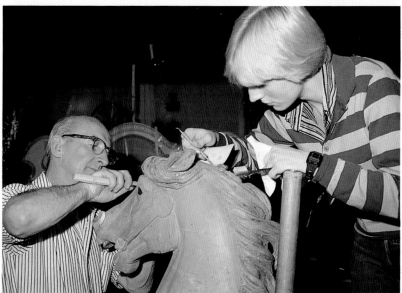

Careful stripping
reveals the original paint
details on one of
Looff's early ponies,
"Angel."

Ears and legs are very
vulnerable to damage.
Wood-carver Terry
Causgrove works on an
ear, while restorer
Lynda Oakley works
on the stripping process.

A restorer applies a
touch of gold on a Looff
horse.

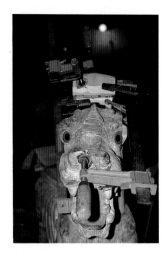

Glued and clamped,
Carlsbad the dragon
suffers repairs to its
badly damaged body.

Carol Perron and Roger
Sogge (above right)
plan the reconstruction
of the batwing saddle
removed by a former
owner from the
Looff dragon that is to
go aboard the Portland
Looff carousel.

Roger Sogge (right)
carefully builds up the
dragon's saddle with
blocks of basswood.

Roger Sogge carves
the final details on
Carlsbad's saddle
(right).

Back on the carousel,
Carlsbad is awesome,
and shows no hint of the
seemingly hopeless
shape it was in before
restoration (far right).

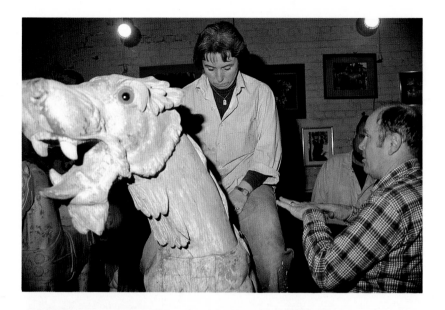

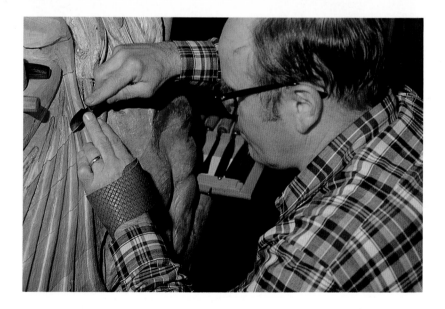

A large, beautifully painted Arab portrait is part of the trappings on the P.T.C. #6 camel at Burlington, Colorado.

The lavish flowers and trappings on this horse on the carousel in Spokane's Riverfront Park (above right) are examples of the more elaborate decorations Looff carved.

At the outset, one couple had named their outside-row stander "Falstaff" (because the man drove a beer truck and, as they explained, "Falstaff is a more fitting name for a knight's horse than Budweiser"). When they finished scraping off thick coats of ugly paint they discovered that the face peering out from the saddle cantle had a Falstaffian grin, complete with a red nose (red paint soaks into wood and leaves a stain) and a rakish beret.

The hollow bodies of some animals held small treasures dropped in by children as they gripped the brass poles many generations ago. Coins gave clues for identifying dates. Tickets showed ride prices and cities and towns where the animals had been.

No other discovery quite matched the dainty woman's watch found in one animal, but there were some unusual finds. One horse's body was stuffed with ancient, blackened straw. The mystery of how it got there was solved when a coral-hued feather emerged. Finally, a tiny woodpecker skeleton was found. It seemed only proper to give the horse the name "Lady Nester."

Most of the animals desperately needed repairs. Years of carrying riders had loosened joints; ears, nostrils, and manes were chipped or broken; and whole legs were missing. Old breaks had often been patched with soft metal plates or with pincushions of rusted nails whose shape often indicated the era in which the repair had been made. A group of volunteers from the local woodcarvers' association devoted hundreds of hours to whittling replacements and to gluing, doweling, filling, and making generally battered animals whole again.

The most dramatic rescue was that of a fine Looff dragon that had been severely damaged by floods. Its former owner, who operated an Upstate New York amusement park, had given up trying to repair it and installed it in the park's fun house. Battered as it was and glowing with garish fluorescent paint, the huge dragon had a dignity and personality that captivated everyone who saw it. Its batwing saddle and topknot needed complete rebuilding. Its gracefully curling tail had to be redoweled, glued, and fitted securely. To remove scars and dents that covered every inch of its body required days of filling and sanding followed by many coats of new paint. The project took months.

The resurrected dragon is the most eye-catching figure on the completed carousel. Looking at it today, you could not guess the many hours of painstaking work that went into its rebirth.

The Looff mechanism needed a complete overhauling. The sweeps and other wooden parts had to be scraped and repainted. The electrical system had to be brought up to current code. No rounding boards existed, so new ones had to be designed and built, again by volunteers, who—for each of the sixteen sections—constructed and assembled more than two hundred wooden parts, plus electrical fittings. Later, a new deck had to be built.

The newly refurbished carousel was rededicated in a colorful ceremony during the 1982 National Carousel Association convention in Portland, Oregon, where it has spun its magic for riders almost daily in the years since the restoration.

Wendell Warren cleans up old paint on a mirrored Looff rounding board to be displayed at the International Museum of Carousel Art.

Terry Medaris puts
final touches of
paint on the massive
lovers' chariot
from P.T.C. #15.

Present Plans and Future Fancies

E l Dorado is a splendid 3-tiered, 60-foot in diameter, 150-passenger carousel that was built in Leipzig, Germany, and shipped to Coney Island in 1902. It is one of the few carousels ever imported into the United States. A 1951 *Life* magazine article predicted that "it will probably still be spinning when fads like the Atomic Bomber have yielded to the Interplanetary Dipsy-Doodle." The magazine's crystal ball failed to reveal that El Dorado would be sold in the early 1970s to Toshimaen Amusement Park in Tokyo, Japan, where it still casts its spell of enchantment on riders.

The sweeping changes that have occurred at an accelerating pace over the past century have had their effect on the glittery world of the amusement park. Although the carousel and the amusement park still provide Americans with a few hours of escape from reality, the number of parks, and of carousels, diminishes every year. Rising land values, insurance costs, and operating expenses are taking their toll.

More and more people are beginning to appreciate the superb craftsmanship in the best of the venerable carousels and are aware of the threats to carousels as an endangered species. Carousels have been put back into operation as drawing cards in malls and other commercial developments. Many have found homes in city parks, where they are under the protection of local governments or volunteer groups that keep them from being dismantled and sold at

How many of the carousels still intact today will survive the 1990s? And how many of the amusement parks we enjoy will still be around for the next generation's pleasure? The crystal ball can show us only a blurred view of the future of the carousel and the amusement park.

This silver-gray Dentzel was photographed while on exhibit at the Mingei Museum of Folk Art in La Jolla, California. The horse's owners are William H. and Marion Dentzel of Santa Barbara, California.

auction houses to collectors. Under civic ownership they are less susceptible than in an amusement park to the need for every square foot to pay its way.

Meanwhile, people's nostalgia for bygone days shows no sign of waning. In a world suffering from the future shock of too-rapid change, the past offers a solid anchor. Long-ignored old homes and office buildings, shabby urban historic districts, and the decaying centers of small towns are being refurbished and cherished as talismans of a stable society. Carousels and amusement parks are vital parts of this civic renaissance.

Large theme parks attract many millions of visitors each year to see technology at its most ingenious. You can view worlds of the

**King Arthur's carousel,
Disneyland, Anaheim,
California.**

21st century—or of the 19th. In his Tomorrowlands, and in his dream of Epcot, Walt Disney boldly envisioned a future not just for the space traveler or the physicist but for Mr. and Mrs. Average American and their family. Disney's dreams have had an important influence on America. By a strange twist, the idealized Main Streets of his parks have inspired the rebuilding of many real Main Streets in cities and towns in every part of the country.

Both Disneyland and Walt Disney World have old wooden carousels, as do most other established theme parks. A more recently opened theme park, Dollywood, has leased a fine old Dentzel menagerie that last operated at Lake Lansing, Michigan. It is the focal point of the park's Victorian-themed village, just inside the park's entrance.

Not many parks today are so successful in finding an authentic wooden carousel. Too few are available. Some parks import, mostly from Italy, new mass-produced carousels with elaborate decorations but with characterless fiberglass animals. The Chance Manufacturing Company recently began offering another option. It is creating ornate carousel replicas in fiberglass from molds made by Bradley & Kaye of Long Beach, California, of the finest antique figures, scenery panels, and rounding boards.

What will the next century hold? Will future generations be able to enjoy amusement parks? There will obviously continue to be changes, but it is hard to tell what form they will take. One trend is toward the family entertainment center—an amusement park environment built into a shopping mall that may offer a small

Dentzel carousel, Weona Park, Pen Argyl, Pennsylvania.

Carol's Carousel, Portland, Oregon.

Carol's Carousel, Portland, Oregon.

fiberglass carousel as a drawing card. Another trend is toward the total shopping-dining-recreation environment like that of the gigantic Edmonton Mall in Alberta, Canada.

The elegant centerpiece for the Pyramid Conpanies' enormous new Carousel Center is P.T.C. #18, built in 1909, and restored after running for years at the now defunct Roseland Park in Canandaigua, New York. It has returned to a former home, the site of another vanished park, Long Branch on Onondaga Lake near Syracuse.

Although futurists predict a continuing increase in the amount of available leisure time, you will not find many of then who give any thought to how that time might be spent. The future of the carousel and the amusement park, like recreation in general, is being ignored.

The amusement park in an overpopulated future would have to become smaller. Today's sprawling landscape of rides may be

replaced by compact, simulated ones, in which the rider is seated in a small room designed to give the dizzying sensations of a ride on a roller coaster, a Loop-a-Plane, or an Octopus. The idea is not a new one. "A Trip to the Moon" was an instant hit at the 1901 Pan-American Exposition in Buffalo, New York. Japan has been successfully using roller coaster "mental rides" for some years.

While the feel of many rides can be successfully simulated, that of the antique carousel presents a more complex problem. To lose yourself in its fantasy, you must sit astride a real wooden animal and open yourself to the aura of the thousands of riders who have sat in that saddle. It is not merely a visual effect; your imagination must play a part. And that is much more difficult to simulate than a wild roller coaster ride.

In "My Amusement Park of the Future," which was a chapter in Tim Onosko's book *Funland U.S.A.,* the noted science writer Isaac Asimov foresees in an even more distant future the possibility of amusement parks on low-gravity planets or on specially built orbiting satellites. Or if the population goes underground to inhabit a climate-controlled subterranean world, the thrill might

■

Carousel Museums

Carousel museums have opened in various parts of the country within the past few years. These are excellent places to learn more about the carousel's history and tradition. Most also have shops that sell carousel art, books, and memorabilia.

The Carousel Society of the Niagara Frontier's museum is housed in an old Herschell factory building in North Tonawanda, New York. Inside the building you can ride a three-row 1916 Allan Herschell carousel with inner rows of earlier Herschell-Spillman horses.

The International Museum of Carousel Art in Portland, Oregon, opened as the Portland Carousel Museum in 1984. Part of the fun of a Portland visit is riding the city's five operating antique carousels, outstanding examples of the variety of styles of four American carving shops and one British builder.

The American Carousel Museum at Fisherman's Wharf in San Francisco offers antique animals for sale and gives restoration demonstrations.

The New England Carousel Museum opened in Bristol, Connecticut, in 1989. It has both permanent exhibits and displays from private collections. It is on the ground floor of R&F Designs. You can watch carving restoration and machinery repair work in progress on the second floor.

come from visiting the green surface of the earth to enjoy a closeness to nature and to encounter the phenomena of weather and wilderness.

In such a time, both traditional amusement parks and today's theme parks would be merely memories. To help future generations in such a world savor and understand something of entertainment in the twentieth century, we are obliged to preserve the old wooden carousels that are part of our heritage.

The carousel's Golden Age ended forever half a century ago. Yet, as long as there are people who care enough to preserve, restore, operate, and ride the magnificent remnants of that age, the spirit of the carousel will not fade. Hop aboard a painted pony and travel back to a simpler yesterday, giving your fantasies free rein—all for the price of a ticket.

The Shelburne Museum in Shelburne, Vermont, has on exhibit horses, menagerie animals, and scenery panels from its 1903 Dentzel carousel, as well as an operating two-row Herschell-Spillman carousel.

At the spacious carousel building at Sea Breeze in Rochester, New York, in addition to taking a ride on P.T.C. #36, you can see a carving museum, with a Lochman carving machine, and two operating miniature carousels.

Another carousel museum has recently opened in the old post office building in Sandusky, Ohio, where the United States Postal Service celebrated the first day of issue in October 1988 of the block of four carousel stamps.

Many other carousel buildings display collections of photographs, plans, and memorabilia relating to the history of their carousel.

King Arthur's Carousel, Disneyland, Anaheim, California.

127

Looff lion, owned by Carol and Duane Perron, on exhibit at the World Forestry Center, Portland, Oregon.

Horses from Carol's Carousel, Portland, Oregon. Do they romp after hours when everyone has left the park?

Floyd L. Moreland was sure when he was a very young boy that he wanted to run this Dentzel mixed carousel at Seaside Heights, New Jersey. He operated it summers during his college years, and later, on weekends and vacations, after he became a professor of Latin and Greek. He has organized friends and relatives to refurbish it and opened A Magical Carousel Gift Shop next to it. In 1986 the carousel was renamed the Floyd L. Moreland Carousel in his honor.

Carol's Carousel, Portland, Oregon.

The Prospect Park carousel in Brooklyn, New York (top and left), is currently being restored to its original splendor. The carousel, which dates back to the early 1900s and has more than fifty animals, is the work of noted carver Charles Carmel.

Carousel Chronology

The easiest and most graphic way to get a picture of "what" and "when" in the carousel industry is with a chronological table. Some dates can only be given approximately, but they are close enough to show the events that led to the Golden Age of the Carousel and then the decline of the industry.

1705   Thomas Newcomen, England, designed the atmospheric steam engine.

1769   James Watt, Scotland, designed the first modern steam condensing engine.

1784   Carousels were outlawed by action of the New York City Common Council.

1805   Joseph Marie Jacquard, France, invented the Jacquard loom, using punched cardboard "books" to weave patterned cloth automatically.

1837   Michael Dentzel, Germany, built his first carousel.

1845   A. F. Setyre obtained a patent to apply the Jacquard principle to musical instruments.

1846   Gustav Dentzel was born in Kreuznach, Germany.

1846   Lake Compounce, Bristol, Connecticut, opened as an amusement park. It was owned by the same family until 1985. Now called Lake Compounce Festival Park, it has operated longer than any other American park.

1850   Eliphalet Scripture of Green Point, New York, was granted the first American carousel patent. Scripture also designed the first overhead carousel propulsion system.

1851   Allan Herschell was born in Scotland.

1852   Charles I. D. Looff was born in Schleswig-Holstein.

1853   Exhibition of the Industry of All Nations in New York City. A bucket-seat carousel was operated at the Crystal Palace.

1853   Rudolph Wurlitzer came to the U.S. from Germany.

1855   Joshua C. Stoddard (United States) invented the calliope. It never caught on in Europe.

1856 The House of Wurlitzer was founded in Cincinnati, Ohio.

1864 Gustav Dentzel immigrated to the U.S. and settled in the Germantown section of Philadelphia.

1864 Charles Wallace Parker was born in Griggsville, Illinois.

1865 Charles Carmel was born in Russsia.

1867 Gustav Dentzel opened his first carousel shop in Germantown, Pennsylvania. He built his first carousel (the first park machine in America) and installed it on Smith Island in the Delaware River near Philadelphia.

1867 William F. Mangels was born in Germany.

1867 Harry Goldstein was born in Russia.

c. 1868 Gustav Dentzel installed his second carousel in Atlantic City, New Jersey.

1870 Frederick Savage, King's Lynn, England, invented the center truck and produced the first steam-propelled carousel.

1870 Charles I. D. Looff immigrated to the U.S., settling in Brooklyn, New York.

1870 Allan Herschell immigrated to the U.S., settling in Buffalo, New York.

1871 Marcus Charles Illions was born in Russia.

1872 Daniel C. Muller was born in Germany.

1872 Allan Herschell, James Armitage, and Alexander Kent founded the Tonawanda Engine & Machine Co.

1875 Charles I. D. Looff began carving his first carousel in his spare time while working in a Brooklyn furniture factory.

1876 William H. (Billy) Dentzel was born in Philadelphia.

1876 Looff's first carousel, a menagerie, was installed at Balmer's Pavilion, Coney Island, Brooklyn, New York.

1876 Armitage and Herschell relocated to North Tonawanda and formed the Armitage-Hershell Company.

1879 Salvatore Cernigliaro was born in Palermo, Italy.

1880 Beginning of the Great Immigration: millions of people migrated from Europe to the U.S.; it lasted until about 1914.

c. 1880 The beginning of the Golden Age of the Carousel.

1881 The Henry Muller family, with sons Daniel and Alfred, arrived in the U.S. from Germany and settled in Philadelphia.

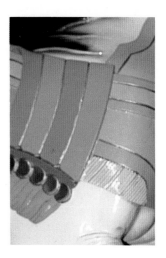

1882 Solomon Stein was born in Russia.

1883 Allan Herschell built his first Steam Riding Gallery.

1883 Charles Carmel and William F. Mangels immigrated to the U.S.; both settled in Brooklyn, New York.

1883 Amusement rides were first opened at Dorney Park, Allentown, Pennsylvania.

■

1884 The first electric trolley car began operation.

1885 Marcus Charles Illions left Russia for Germany; he then went to England, where he worked for Frederick Savage.

1888 Frederick Savage invented the jumping (or galloping) mechanism for carousels.

1888 Marcus Charles Illions arrived in the U.S., settling in Brooklyn, New York.

c. 1890 The Bungarz Stage, Wagon and Carousel Works was founded.

1891 The first American band organ was produced by the North Tonawanda Barrel Organ Factory in North Tonawanda, New York.

1891 The Allan Herschell Company claimed to be shipping carousels at the rate of one per day.

1892 Charles Wallace Parker produced his first carousel.

1892 Lidovico Gavioli built the first book organ in Paris.

c. 1893 Charles Wallace Parker founded the Parker Carnival Supply Company in Abilene, Kansas.

1893 World's Columbian Exposition, Chicago.

1898 The American Merry-Go-Round and Novelty Company was formed.

c. 1900 Paper rolls became popular for band organs.

1901 C. W. F. Dare died, and the New York Carousel Mfg. Company shut down.

1901 Wm. F. Mangels patented an improved galloping mechanism.

1902 M. C. Illions and William F. Mangels rebuilt the fire-damaged Feltman carousel at Coney Island.

1902 Harry Goldstein immigrated to America, settling in Brooklyn, New York.

1902 Salvatore Cernigliaro immigrated to America. He worked first for E. Joy Morris carving carousel animals and then was hired by Gustav Dentzel.

1903 Daniel Carl Muller and Alfred Muller founded the D. C. Muller & Bro. Company to build carousels.

1903 Harry B. Auchy and Chester E. Albright incorporated the Philadelphia Toboggan Company.

1903 Herschell-Spillman bought out the Armitage-Herschell assets and began manufacturing carousels.

1903 Solomon Stein immigrated to America, settling in Brooklyn, New York.

1904 The Philadelphia Toboggan Company turned out the first five of their numbered carousels. All five were three-row machines.

1904 The Louisiana Purchase Exposition in St. Louis celebrated the 100th anniversary of the opening of the West. The Parker carousel now at Jantzen Beach, Portland, Oregon, is reputed to have operated at that exposition.

1905   Charles I. D. Looff moved his factory to Riverside, Rhode Island.

1905   The Philadelphia Toboggan Company produced P.T.C. #6 for Elitch Gardens in Denver, Colorado. That carousel is now in Burlington, Colorado.

1905   Philipps, in Frankfurt, Germany, invented the automatic band organ roll changer.

1907   The Philadelphia Toboggan Company produced P.T.C. #15, the first four-row, all-jumper carousel, for Wendell's Park, Fort George, New York.

1907   The Philadelphia Toboggan Company produced P.T.C. #17, the first five-row carousel, for Chicago's Riverview Park. The carousel is now at Six Flags Over Georgia.

1907   William F. Mangels of Coney Island designed and patented an improved jumping mechanism for the carousel.

1907   Rudolph Wurlitzer's factory produced its first band organs.

1908   M. C. Illions and Sons was established in Brooklyn, New York.

1909   Gustav Dentzel died; William H. ("Billy") Dentzel took over the company.

1909   Henry Auchy patented his new friction drive for propelling carousels.

1910   Charles I. D. Looff moved his factory to Long Beach, California.

c. 1910   Charles Carmel opened his carving shop in Brooklyn, New York.

1911   John Zalar joined the Looff factory.

1911   The Parker Carnival Supply Company moved operations to Leavenworth, Kansas.

1911   Allan Herschell sold his interest in the Herschell-Spillman Company.

1911   Dreamland Park, Coney Island, burned to the ground.

1912   Solomon Stein, Harry Goldstein, and Henry Dorber organized the Artistic Carousel Manufacturers.

c. 1912   The use of the Lochman carving machine changed carving styles and production methods in some carousel shops.

c. 1912   Frank Carretta was hired by the Philadelphia Toboggan Company.

1913   The San Diego Exposition carousel was a 1906 Dentzel, four-row. (It was partially destroyed by fire in 1958. The remaining pieces were sold individually.)

1914   The Great Immigration from Europe to the U.S. ended.

1915   Allan Herschell, with two partners, started the Allan Herschell Co.

1915   San Francisco's Panama-Pacific International Exposition had a carousel from the 1913 San Diego Exposition; also an English roundabout (now at Oak Meadows Park, Los Gatos, California).

1916   The probable date the last Looff carousel was built.

1916   John Zalar was employed by the Philadelphia Toboggan Company.

1917   The Muller brothers closed shop.

1918   Stein & Goldstein closed their carousel shop.

1918   Charles I. D. Looff died.

c. 1918   Charles Carmel closed his carousel shop.

1920   Herschell-Spillman was reorganized as Spillman Engineering.

1923   Allan Herschell resigned as president of the Allan Herschell Co.

1924   The last Dentzel carousel was built. It is now at Six Flags Over Texas, having been moved from Rockaway's Playland, Rockaway Beach, Long Island.

1928   William H. (Billy) Dentzel died and the Dentzel Company was sold at auction.

1928 & 1929   Frank Carretta won the National Association of Amusement Parks carving contests.

1929   William F. Mangels founded the American Museum of Public Recreaton at Coney Island.

c. 1930   The Golden Age of the Carousel ended.

1932   Charles Carmel died.

1933–34   Chicago's Century of Progress Exposition.

1934   Charles Wallace Parker died.

c. 1934   The Philadelphia Toboggan Company built its last carousel.

1939–40   San Francisco's Golden Gate International Exposition. The carousel was the c. 1912 Herschell-Spillman from Griffith Park, Los Angeles; it was moved to Portland, Oregon's Lotus Isle; then to Treasure Island, San Francisco, for the 1940 Golden Gate Exposition; then to the Children's Playground in San Francisco's Golden Gate Park, where it is still in operation.

1939–40   New York's World of Tomorrow world's fair.

1945   The Allan Herschell Company bought out the Spillman Engineering Corp.

1945   Harry Goldstein died.

1949   Marcus Charles Illions died.

1952   Daniel Muller died.

1954   The Theel Manufacturing Company bought out the Parker Company.

1955   The American Museum of Public Recreation closed its doors.

1958   The 1906 Dentzel carousel from the San Diego Exposition, San Francisco's Panama Pacific Exposition, and Neptune Beach, Alameda, California, was partially destroyed by fire; the remaining pieces were sold individually.

1970   The Allan Herschell Company was bought out by Chance Manufacturing Company.

1973   The National Carousel Roundtable (now the National Carousel Association) was organized.

1974   The First National Carousel Roundtable conference was held in Sandwich, Massachusetts.

Carousels and Parks

Disneyland, 1313 Harbor Blvd., Anaheim, California 92803

Tilden Park, Berkeley, California 94708; 415-524-6283

Knott's Berry Farm, 8039 Beach Blvd., Buena Park, California 90620 (from Hersheypark, Hershey, PA)

Shoreline Village, 407 Village Drive, Long Beach, California 90802; 213-435-5911 (from Playland-at-the-Beach, San Francisco)

Griffith Park, Park Center, Los Angeles, California; 213-665-3051 (from Mission Beach, San Diego)

Balboa Park, Zoo Place at Park Blvd., San Diego, California 92101; 714-460-9000 (from Tent City, Coronado, and Luna Park, Los Angeles)

Broadway Flying Horses, Seaport Village, 849 W. Harbor Drive, San Diego, California 92101; 619-235-4014 (from Coney Island, then Salisbury Beach, MA)

San Francisco Zoo Carousel, Sloat Blvd. off 45th Ave., San Francisco, California 94132

Golden Gate Park, San Francisco, California 94131; 415-558-4249

Santa Cruz Beach Boardwalk, 400 Beach St., Santa Cruz, California 95060; 408-423-5590 (in original location)

Santa Monica Pier Carousel, end of Colorado Avenue, Santa Monica, California 90401; 213-458-8698 (from Cumberland Park, Nashville, TN)

Kit Carson County Fairgrounds, Burlington, Colorado 80807; 303-346-5275 (from Elitch Gardens, Denver)

Elitch Gardens, 4620 W. 38th Ave., Denver, Colorado 80212; 303-455-4771 (original location)

Lakeside Park, 4601 Sheridan Blvd., Denver, Colorado 80212; 303-477-1621

Pueblo City Park, 800 Goodnight Ave., Pueblo, Colorado 81005; 303-566-1745 (from Lake Minnequa, Pueblo)

Bushnell Park, Jewell & Trinity Sts., Hartford, Connecticut 06103; 203-738-3089 (from Meyer's Lake Park, Canton, OH)

Washington National Cathedral, Wisconsin and Massachusetts Aves., NW, Washington, D.C.; 202-537-6200 (operates only two days per year)

Six Flags Over Georgia, I-20 West, Atlanta, Georgia 30378; 404-948-9290 (from Riverview Park, Chicago, IL)

Kiddieland, 8400 West North Ave., Melrose Park, Illinois 60160; 312-343-1050 (from Waterbury, CT, and Delaware Beach)

Electric Park, Morgantown, Indiana (to open in 1990s)

Palace Playland, 1 Old Orchard St., Old Orchard Beach, Maine 04084; 207-934-2001 (from Euclid Beach, Cleveland, OH)

Glen Echo Park, MacArthur Blvd. and Route 614, Glen Echo, Maryland 20812; 301-492-6266 (original location)

Watkins Regional Park, Largo, Maryland 20772; 301-249-9325 (from Chesapeake Beach)

Trimpers Rides/Windsor Resort, Ocean City, Maryland 21842; 301-289-8617 (original location)

Riverside Park, 1623 Main St., Agawam, Massachusetts 01001; 413-786-9300

Carousel Under the Clock, Hull, Massachusetts 02045 (from Paragon Park, Hull)

Flying Horses, New York Ave., Oak Bluffs, Martha's Vineyard, Massachusetts 02557; 617-693-9481

Heritage Plantation, Sandwich, Massachusetts 02563; 617-888-3300 (from Coney Island, moved to Oak Bluffs in 1890s)

Edaville Railroad, Route 58, South Carver, Massachusetts 02336; 617-866-4526

Greenfield Village, Henry Ford Museum, Oakwood Blvd., Dearborn, Michigan 48121; 313-271-1620

Historical Crossroads Village, G-6140 Bray, Flint, Michigan 48506; 313-763-7100 (from Fairmont City Park, Riverside, CA, and Washington Park, El Paso, TX)

Dutch Village, U.S. 31 at James, Holland, Michigan 49424; 616-399-1475

Highland Park, State Blvd., Meridian, Mississippi 39301; 601-485-1801

Clementon Lake Amusement Park, 144 Berlin Road, Clementon, New Jersey 08021; 609-783-0263 (original location)

Six Flags Great Adventure, Rte. 357, Jackson, New Jersey 08527; 201-928-2000

Wonderland Pier, Boardwalk and 6th St., Ocean City, New Jersey 08226; 609-399-7082 (from Dallas, PA; Rolling Green Park, Sellinsgrove, PA)

The Floyd L. Moreland Carousel, Casino Pier, Boardwalk and Sherman, Seaside Heights, New Jersey 08751; 201-830-4183

Spring River Park, College and Atkinson Sts., Roswell, New Mexico; 505-622-5811

Nunley's Carousel, 850 Sunrise Highway, Baldwin, New York 11510; 516-223-4742 (from Canarsie Beach, Brooklyn)

George F. Johnson Recreational Park, Beethoven St., Binghamton, New York 13905; 607-722-9166 (original location)

Ross Park Zoo, Ross Park, Binghamton, New York 13903; 607-724-5454 (original location)

B & B Carousel, Surf Ave. and West 10th St., Coney Island, Brooklyn, New York 11224

Prospect Park, Flatbush Ave. and Ocean Ave., Brooklyn, New York 11225 (from Coney Island in 1952)

George W. Johnson Park, Oak Hill Ave. at Witherill St., Endicott, New York 13760 (original location)

C. Fred Johnson Park, Lester Ave. at CFJ Blvd., Johnson City, New York 13790 (original location)

Central Park, 65th St. and Center Drive, New York, New York 10021; 212-744-9779 (from Coney Island)

Carousel Society of the Niagara Frontier, 180 Thompson St., North Tonawanda, New York 14120; 716-693-1885

Ontario Beach Park, Lake Ave., Charlotte, Rochester, New York 14612; 716-244-4640

Sea Breeze Park, 4600 Culver Road, Rochester, New York 14622; 716-467-3422

Rye Playland Park, Playland Parkway, Rye, New York 10580; 914-967-2040

Carousel Center, Syracuse, New York, 315-422-7000 (from Long Branch, Syracuse, then Roseland Park, Canandaigua)

Highland Avenue Park, Union, Broome County, New York 13760 (original location)

West Endicott Park, Page Ave., Union, Broome County, New York 13760 (from En Joie Park, Endicott)

Burlington City Park, Burlington, North Carolina 27215; 919-226-7371 (from Forest Park, Genoa, OH)

Chavis Park, Raleigh, North Carolina 27602; 919-755-6640

Wyandot Amusement Park, 10101 N. Riverside Dr., Columbus, Ohio 43065; 614-889-8465 (from Olentangy Park, Columbus)

Tuscora Park, Tuscora Ave. NW, New Philadelphia, Ohio 44663; 216-343-4644

Cedar Point, Sandusky, Ohio 44870; 419-627-2284 (five carousels)

Carol's Carousel, Washington Park, 4033 SW Canyon Road, Portland, Oregon 97221; 503-228-1367

Jantzen Beach Center, 1492 Jantzen Beach Drive, Portland, Oregon 97217; 503-289-5555 (from Jantzen Beach Amusement Park)

Oaks Park, East End of Sellwood Bridge, Portland, Oregon 97202; 503-233-5777 (original location)

Portland Looff Carousel, Carousel Courtyard, NE Holladay between 7th and 9th, Portland, Oregon 97232; 503-230-0400 (from Fair Park, TX; P.O.P., Santa Monica, CA; Spanaway, WA)

Albion Boro Park, Albion, Pennsylvania 16401 (from Lorain, OH)

Dorney Park, 3830 Dorney Park Road, Allentown, Pennsylvania (Dentzel carousel being restored in Connecticut)

Bushkill Park, 2125 Bushkill Park Drive, Easton, Pennsylvania 18042; 215-258-6941

Knoebels Amusement Resort, Rte. 487, Elysburg, Pennsylvania 17824; 717-672-2572 (two carousels)

Hersheypark, 100 W. Hersheypark Drive, Hershey, Pennsylvania 17033; 717-534-3900 (from Liberty Heights Park, Baltimore, MD; Auburn, NY)

Idlewild Park, Ligonier, Pennsylvania 15658; 412-238-9881

Weona Park, Rte. 512, Pen Argyl, Pennsylvania 18072; 215-863-9249

Bland's Park, Tipton, Pennsylvania 16684; 814-943-5304

Kennywood, 4800 Kennywood Blvd., West Mifflin, Pennsylvania 15122; 412-461-0500 (near Pittsburgh) (original location)

Crescent Park, Bullocks Point Avenue, Providence, Rhode Island 02915; 401-434-3311 Ext. 297 (original location)

Watch Hill Flying Horses, Westerly, Rhode Island 02891

Lagoon Amusement Park, Farmington, Utah 84025; 801-451-0101 (north of Salt Lake City)

Bickleton Merry-Go-Round, Bickleton, Washington 99322

Riverfront Park Carousel, N. 507 Howard St., Spokane, Washington 99206; 509-456-5512 (from Natatorium Park, Spokane)

Carousel Museums

•

The Carousel Society of the
Niagara Frontier (museum and
carousel), 180 Thompson St.,
North Tonawanda, New York
14120; 716-693-1885

The International Museum of
Carousel Art (museum and
carousel), NE Holladay St. at
7th, Portland, Oregon 97232;
503-230-0400

The American Carousel Museum,
Beach St., San Francisco, California

The New England Carousel
Museum, 11 Prospect St., Bristol, Connecticut 06010

The Shelburne Museum (museum
and carousel), Shelburne, Vermont 05482; 802-985-3346

Parks and/or Carousels
No Longer in Existence

•

Pacific Ocean Park, Santa Monica,
California (park gone; Looff
carousel in Portland, Oregon)

Lake Quassy, Route 64, Middlebury, Connecticut (carousel
auctioned and broken up October 21, 1989)

Riverview Park, Chicago, Illinois
(park gone; P.T.C. #17
carousel at Six Flags Over Georgia, Atlanta)

Vinewood Park, Topeka, Kansas
(park gone; P.T.C. carousel
broken up long ago)

North Beach, Queens, New York
(park gone; fate of carousel unknown)

Seneca Park, Rochester, New
York (park gone; Long carousel
destroyed by fire)

Idora Park, Youngstown, Ohio
(park closed; carousel being restored in Brooklyn)

Lakemont Park, Altoona, Pennsylvania (carousel broken up at
auction)

Waldameer Park, Erie, Pennsylvania (carousel broken up at
auction)

Chestnut Hill, Philadelphia, Pennsylvania (park gone; fate of
carousel unknown)

Fairmount Park, Philadelphia,
Pennsylvania (park gone; fate of
carousel unknown)

Fun Forest, Seattle Center, Seattle, Washington (carousel
broken up at auction in 1989)

Crystal Beach, Ontario, Canada
(park closed in 1989; carousel
broken up at auction earlier)

Bibliography

Amusement Parks and Fairs

•

Braithwaite, David. *Fairground Architecture, the World of Amusement Parks, Carnivals and Fairs.* New York: Frederick A. Praeger, 1978.

Brown, Jeff, and Ray Fete. *Meyer's Lake, A Second Look.* Canton, Ohio: Daring Books, 1988.

Carlson, Raymond, ed. *National Directory of Theme Parks and Amusement Areas.* New York: Pilot Books, 1978.

Francis, David W., and Diane DeMali Francis. *Cedar Point: The Queen of American Watering Places.* Canton, Ohio: Daring Books, 1988.

Griffin, Al. *Step Right Up, Folks.* Chicago: Henry Regnery Co., 1974.

Hilton, Suzanne. *Here Today and Gone Tomorrow, The Story of World's Fairs and Expositions.* Philadelphia: The Westminster Press, 1978.

Hunter, Susan. *A Family Guide to Amusement Centers.* New York: Walker & Company, 1975.

Jacques, Charles J., Jr. *Kennywood.* Vestal, N.Y.: The Vestal Press, 1982.

Kasson, John F. *Amusing the Million, Coney Island at the Turn of the Century.* New York: Hill & Wang, 1978.

Kyriazi, Gary. *The Great American Amusement Parks, a Pictorial History.* Secaucus, N.J.: Citadel Press, 1976.

Luckhurst, Kenneth W. *The Story of Exhibitions.* New York: The Studio Publications, 1951.

Mangels, William F. *The Outdoor Amusement Industry: From the Earliest Times to the Present.* New York: Vantage Press, 1952.

McCauley, Peter, ed. *Boulevard Landmarks: Greetings from Revere Beach.* Revere, Mass: Peter McCauley, 1988.

———. *A Pictorial History of Revere Beach,* vol 1. Revere, Mass.: Peter McCauley, 1980. Revised 1986.

Onosko, Tim. *Funland U.S.A. The Complete Guide to 100 Major Amusement and Theme Parks.* New York: Ballantine Books, 1978.

Paschen, Stephen. *Shootin' the Chutes: Amusement Parks Remembered.* Akron, Ohio: The Summit County Historical Society, 1988.

Pilat, Oliver, and Jo Ranson. *Sodom by the Sea: the Affectionate History of Coney Island.* Garden City, N.Y.: Doubleday, Doran & Company, 1941.

Reed, James W. *The Top 100 Amusement Parks of the United States; the 1978 Guidebook to Amusement Parks.* Quarryville, Penn.: Reed Publishing Company, 1978.

Stanton, Jeffrey. *Venice of America: Coney Island of the Pacific.* Los Angeles: Donahue Publishing, 1987.

Ulmer, Jeff. *Amusement Parks of America, A Comprehensive Guide.* New York: The Dial Press, 1980.

Williams, Barbara, and Sara Cancholsa. *The Flying Horses: A Pictorial History of Southern California's Carousels.* Los Angeles: National Carousel Association, 1978.

■

Winfield, Barbara LaBarge. *The Carvers and Their Merry-Go-Rounds*. Text by Tina Cristiani Gottdenker. West Babylon, N.Y.: National Carousel Roundtable, 1974.

Folk Art

•

American Folk Art: Expressions of a New Spirit. New York: Museum of American Folk Art, 1983.

Ayres, James. *British Folk Art*. London: Overlook Press, 1977.

Carrington, Noel. *Popular English Art*. Illustrated by Clarke Hutton. New York: King Penguin Books, 1945.

Christensen, Erwin O. *Early American Wood Carving*. New York: Dover Publications, 1952.

————. *Index of American Design*. New York: Macmillan Co., 1950.

Comstock, Helen, ed. *Concise Encyclopedia of American Antiques*. New York: Hawthorn Books, 1958.

The Craftsman in America. Washington, D.C.: National Geographic Society, 1975.

The Encyclopedia of Collectibles. Alexandria, Va.: Time-Life Books, 1978.

Fried, Fred and Mary. *America's Forgotten Folk Arts*. New York: Pantheon Books, 1978.

Gladstone, M. J. *A Carrot for a Nose*. New York: Charles Scribner's Sons., 1974.

Hornung, Clarence P. *Treasury of American Design*. New York: Harry N. Abrams, 1972.

Jones, Barbara. *The Unsophisticated Arts*. Kent, England: The Architectural Press, 1951.

Klamkin, Charles and Miriam. *Wood Carvings: North American Folk Sculptures*. New York: Hawthorn Books, 1974.

Lipman, Jean. *American Folk Art in Wood, Metal and Stone*. New York: Pantheon Books, 1948.

Treasury of American Antiques, A Pictorial Survey of Popular Folk Art & Crafts. New York: Harry N. Abrams, 1977.

Welsh, Peter C. *American Folk Art: The Art & Spirit of a People*. Washington, D.C.: Smithsonian Institution, 1965.

Band Organs, Music

•

Bowers, Q. David. *Put Another Nickel In*. New York: Bonanza Books, 1966.

Cockayne, Eric V. *The Fairground Organ: Its Music, Mechanism, and History*. Newton Abbott, England: David and Charles Publishers.

————. *The Fair Organ—How It Works: An Introduction to the Mechanical Organ of the Fairground*. St. Albans, England: The Fair Organ Preservation Society, 1967.

de Waard, E. *From Music Boxes to Street Organs*, trans. Wade Jenkins. Vestal, N.Y.: The Vestal Press, 1967.

Ord-Hume, Arthur W. J. G. *Barrel Organ: the Story of the Mechanical Organ and Its Repair*. New York: A. S. Barnes & Co., 1978.

————. *Clockwork Music: An Illustrated History of Mechanical Musical Instruments from the Musical Box to the Pianola, from Automaton Lady Virginal Players to the Orchestrion*. New York: Crown Publishers, 1973.

Reblitz, Arthur, and Q. David Bowers. *Treasures of Mechanical Music*. Vestal, N.Y.: The Vestal Press, 1972.

Roehl, Harvey N. *Player Pianos and Music Boxes: Keys to a Musical Past*. Vestal, N.Y.: The Vestal Press, 1968.

History, Miscellaneous

•

Dickson, Paul. *The Mature Person's Guide to Kites, Yo-Yos, Frisbees and Other Childlike Diversions*. New York: New American Library, 1977.

Goldsack, Bob. *C. W. Parker, the Carnival King*. Nashua, N.H.: Midway Museum Publications, 1988.

Looff Family Photo Memoirs. Garden Grove, Calif.: Cameo Productions, 1982.

Nye, Russel B. *The Cultural Life of the New Nation: 1776 to 1830*. New York: Harper & Brothers, 1960.

————. *The Unembarrassed Muse: The Popular Arts in America*. New York: The Dial Press, 1970.

Stern, Jane and Michael. *Amazing America*. New York: Random House, 1978.

Children's Books

•

Bergeon, JoAnne Medler. *Lions, Tigers & Bears Go 'Round.* Illustrated by Cathy Morrison. Lakewood, Co.: Bookmakers Guild, 1989.

Borzon, Paul Jacques. *The Runaway Flying Horse.* Illustrated by William Pène du Bois. New York: Parents' Magazine Press, 1976.

Brown, Marcia. *The Little Carousel.* New York: Charles Scribner's Sons, 1946.

Cohen, Barbara. *Where's Florrie?* New York: Lothrop, Lee, & Shepard, 1976.

Foster, Elizabeth. *Gigi in America.* Illustrated by Phyllis Cote. Berkeley, Calif.: North Atlantic Books, 1984. (Originally published by Houghton Mifflin, 1946.)

———. *Gigi, The Story of a Carousel Horse.* Illustrated by Ilse Bischoff. Berkeley, Calif.: North Atlantic Books, 1984. (Originally published by Houghton Mifflin, 1943.)

Hayes, Sheila. *The Carousel Horse.* New York: Thomas Y. Nelson, 1979.

Ipcar, Dahlov. *The Marvelous Merry-Go-Round.* Garden City, N.Y.: Doubleday & Co., 1970.

Kroeber, Theodora. *Carrousel.* New York: Atheneum, 1977.

Levenson, Dorothy. *The Magic Carousel.* Illustrated by Ati Forberg. New York: Parents' Magazine Press, 1967.

Martin, Bill, Jr., and John Archambaut. *Up and Down on the Merry-Go-Round.* Illustrated by Ted Rand. New York: Henry Holt and Company, 1988.

McLaughlin, Pat H. *Sabrina and the Island of the Flying Horses.* Illustrated by Joan Maher. El Cajon, Calif.: Pumpkin House Press, 1986.

McSwigan, Marie. *Five on a Merry-Go-Round.* Philadelphia: The Blakiston Co., 1943.

Slobodkin, Louis. *The Adventures of Arab.* New York: The Vanguard Press, 1946.

Smiley, Virginia Kester. *A Horse for Matthew Allen.* Lexington, Mass.: Ginn & Co., 1972.

Thomas, Art. *Merry-Go-Rounds.* Pictures by George Overlie. Minneapolis: Carolrhoda Books, 1981.

Carousels

•

Braithwaite, Paul. *Roundabout: an Investigation of Possible Origins of Roundabouts and Other Riding Machines in the Early Age of Pleasure Fairs.* Private printing, Paul Braithwaite, 1988.

Fraley, Nina. *The American Carousel.* Benecia, Calif.: Redbug Workshop, 1979.

Fried, Frederick. *A Pictorial History of the Carousel.* New York: A. S. Barnes & Co., 1964.

Harris, Cecilia. *Abilene's Carousel.* Abilene, Kans.: Dickinson County Historical Society, no date.

Lantaff, Marion. *The Mesker Park Carousel.* Evansville, Ind.: Lant Graphics, 1981.

Moore, Harriet C. *Around and Around: The Story of the Watch Hill Carousel.* With Lido J. Mochetti. Westerly, R.I.: Sun Graphics, 1980.

Raines, Diane. *Allan Herschell and the Tonawanda Machine: an Exhibition Catalogue.* North Tonawanda, N.Y., the Tonawandas' Council on the Arts, 1980.

Weedon, Goeff, and Richard Ward. *Fairground Art.* New York: Abbeville Press, 1982.

Collecting

•

Dinger, Charlotte. *Art of the Carousel.* Green Village, N.J.: Carousel Art, 1983.

The Encyclopedia of Collectibles, vol. 3, Buttons to Chess Sets. Alexandria, Va.: Time/Life Books, 1978.

Fraley, Tobin. *The Carousel Animal.* Photographs by Gary Sinick. Oakland, Calif.: Zephyr Press, 1983.

Manns, William, Peggy Shank, and Marianne Stevens. *Painted Ponies.* Millwood, N.Y.: Zon International Publishing Co., 1986.

Acknowledgments

Acknowledgments and gratitude to: Norbert Adler, George Appleton, Jean and Ray Auel, Penny Avila, Camellia Barice, Marje Blood, Bill and Marion Dentzel, John Buck, Joe Dion, Carl and Terri Dion, Fred Fried, Charles and Mary Ellen Gardiner, Mona Givens, Gail Hall, Dayton Hyde, Charles J. Jacques, Jr., Connie and Jack Jarvis, Katharine McCanna, Peter McCauley, Brian Morgan, Joan Nelson, Roy Paul Nelson, Paula Nesbitt, Carol and Duane Perron, Nan Phillips, Mark Reed, Jerry and Marilyn Reinhardt, Harvey and Marion Roehl, Opal Stokes, Rol and Jo Summit, Arlene and Peter Ten Eyck, Annie Tuttle, LaVada Weir, and Tracy Weir.

And to The WEB, Lauralee Reinhart, Dave Ulmer, and all the rest; The Oregon Writers Colony; Willamette Writers; Powell's Book Store; Graham's Stationery and Books; Keith Krumbein and Kolour Services; Al Berreth and U-Develop; the Ledding Library of Milwaukie; The Multnomah County Library; and the park and carousel owners across the country, the carousel support groups, and everyone else who has so generously given me helpful information.

And to my agent, Natasha Kern, and to the people at Crown Publishers, my editor, Ann Cahn, Linda Kocur, and Nancy Maynes. And especially all those who have given me hospitality, transportation, and encouragement; who have faithfully sent me information over the years; and whose faith in my ability to finish this book made it possible for me to keep at it.

If you would like to become a member of the NCA, write to:

National Carousel Association
P. O. Box 8115
Zanesville, Ohio 43702-8115

A Guide to the Illustrations

Disneyland, Anaheim, California:
     pages *61, 123, 127, 131*

Tilden Park, Berkeley, California:
     53

Knott's Berry Farm, Buena Park,
     California: *62*

Griffith Park, Los Angeles, Cali-
     fornia: *92, 107*

Rol and Jo Summit, Rolling Hills,
     California: *i, vi, 74, 79,
     126*

Balboa Park, San Diego, Califor-
     nia: *17, 21, 33, 35, 134*

Seaport Village, San Diego, Cali-
     fornia: *x, 61, 77, 91*

Shoreline Village, Long Beach,
     California: *96*

Zoo Carousel, San Francisco, Cali-
     fornia: *19, 97*

William H. Dentzel II, Santa Bar-
     bara, California: *20, 66, 68,
     122*

Santa Monica, California: *83*

Burlington, Colorado: *3, 6, 7, 9,
     46, 47, 49, 87, 89, 101, 118,
     132*

Elitch Gardens, Denver, Colorado:
     13, 137

Lakeside Park, Denver, Colorado:
     27

Pueblo City Park, Pueblo, Col-
     orado: *8, 29, 33*

Bushnell Park, Hartford, Con-
     necticut: *83*

Lake Quassy, Middlebury, Con-
     necticut: *82, 108*

Six Flags Great America, Gurnee,
     Illinois: *133*

Kiddieland, Melrose Park, Illinois:
     81

Harbor Place, Baltimore, Mary-
     land: *121*

Watkins Regional Park, Largo,
     Maryland: *72*

Edaville Railroad, South Carver,
     Massachusetts: *26*

Flying Horses, Martha's Vineyard,
     Massachusetts: *18, 20, 66*

Riverside Park, Agawam, Massa-
     chusetts: *26*

Carousel Under the Clock, Hull,
     Massachusetts: *50, 95*

Greenfield Village, Dearborn,
     Michigan: *24, 62, 71, 136,
     140*

Crossroads Village, Flint, Michi-
     gan: *94*

Dutch Village, Holland, Michigan:
     101

Six Flags Great Adventure, Jack-
     son, New Jersey: *39, 85*

Gillian's Fun Deck, Ocean City,
     New Jersey: *23*

Wonderland Pier, Ocean City,
     New Jersey: *104*

Dr. Floyd L. Moreland Carousel,
     Seaside Heights, New Jersey:
     128

Recreation Park, Binghamton, New
     York: *72*

P.T.C. #61, Brooklyn, New York:
     109

Herschell Carousel Factory, North
     Tonawanda, New York: *70*

Prospect Park, Brooklyn, New
     York: *129*

Ontario Beach, Rochester, New
     York: *141*

Sea Breeze, Rochester, New York:
     75, 111

Rye Playland, Rye, New York: *91*

■

143

Harvey Roehl, Vestal, New York: *102*

Wyandot Lake Park, Columbus, Ohio: *38, 74, 96*

Cedar Point, Sandusky, Ohio: *viii, 30, 32, 41, 55*

Albany, Oregon: *10*

Trolley Museum, Glenwood, Oregon: *41*

Carol's Carousel, Portland, Oregon: *vii, xii, 1, 2, 4, 22, 28, 31, 35, 40, 54, 60, 88, 93, 95, 98, 124, 126, 128*

Duane and Carol Perron, Portland, Oregon: *5, 32, 60, 63, 68, 98, 101, 110, 111, 128*

Jantzen Beach, Portland, Oregon: *80, 90, 92, 112*

Oaks Park, Portland, Oregon: *11, 52*

Portland Looff Carousel, Portland, Oregon: *vi, ix, xi, 38, 57, 78, 103, 110, 114, 115, 116, 117, 118, 119, 137, 138*

P.T.C. #15, Portland, Oregon: *xi, 34, 44, 56, 87, 106, 108, 110, 120, 121*

Rose Festival, Portland, Oregon: *1, 8*

Spooner Roundabout, Portland, Oregon: *103*

Albion Carousel, Albion, Pennsylvania: *82*

Dorney Park, Allentown, Pennsylvania: *vi, 12, 86, 133*

Conneaut Park, Conneaut Lake, Pennsylvania: *141*

Street Merry-Go-Round, Dallastown, Pennsylvania: *36*

Bushkill Park, Easton, Pennsylvania: *14*

Knoebels Amusement Resort, Elysburg, Pennsylvania: *65, 105*

Waldameer Park, Erie, Pennsylvania: *89*

Hersheypark, Hershey, Pennsylvania: *97*

Idlewild Park, Ligonier, Pennsylvania: *iii, 94*

Tuscora Park, New Philadelphia, Ohio: *73*

Weona Park, Pen Argyl, Pennsylvania: *15, 67, 124*

Kennywood Park, West Mifflin, Pennsylvania: *34, 45, 54, 69, 125*

Looff Carousel, East Providence, Rhode Island: *25, 100*

Bickleton, Washington: *58*

Enchanted Forest, Federal Way, Washington: *16*

Fun Forest, Seattle, Washington: *ix, 51*

Riverfront Park, Spokane, Washington: *11, 17, 22, 118, 134, 138, 142*

Canada's Wonderland, Maple, Ontario, Canada: *8*

P.T.C., Skylon Tower, Niagara Falls, Canada: *104*

Port Dalhousie, St. Catharines, Ontario, Canada: *12*

Ferrymead Museum, Christchurch, New Zealand: *100*

Good News

The Holyoke, Massachusetts, carousel (a beautiful P.T.C. in excellent condition) is now owned by the local friends group It will be put back into operation in a new building in a downtown park in that city. It has spent its entire life at Mountain Park, an amusement park in Holyoke, so it is a special joy that it will be able to stay there, despite the financial struggle; economic conditions are not good in that small city right now. This great success makes up for the more usual bad news about carousels being broken up. The carousel's owner sold it to the local group for much less than he had been offered by purchasers who would break it up. He's a real hero!

Photograph Credits

The author wishes to thank the following for permission to use her photographs of them and/or their carousel animals or other materials for this book:

Joanne Brown for the photograph of her on page 89.

Terry Causgrove for the photograph of him on page 115.

Gene Crommett for the photograph of him on page 48.

William H. Dentzel II
William Dentzel II's fish-mouth ring machine on page 20.
Gustav Dentzel factory sign on page 66.
William Dentzel office sign on page 68.
Silver-gray Dentzel, Mingei Museum of Folk Art, La Jolla, California, on page 122.

The Walt Disney Company for the author's pictures of the King Arthur's Carousel, Disneyland, California, on page 61, 123, 127, 131.

Terry Medaris for the photograph of her on page 120.

Dr. Floyd L. Moreland, Casino Pier, Seaside Heights, New Jersey, for the photograph of him on page 128.

Lynda Oakley for the photograph of her on page 115.

Carol and Duane Perron for the many photographs of their carousels, animals, and activities throughout the book, including the restoration and operation of the Portland Looff Carousel, of P.T.C. #15, Carol's Carousel, the Spooner Roundabout, the Coeur d'Alene Carousel, and the Blue Goose; and for her photographs of Duane on page 31 and of Carol on pages 114 and 116.

Merrick Price for the photograph of him on page 26.

Harvey Roehl for the photograph of his fair organ on page 102.

Roger Sogge for the three photographs of him on page 116.

Gary and Delma Sprauer for the photographs of them on page 114.

Rol and Jo Summit, "Flying Horses," Rolling Hills, California, for the photographs of their animals on pages i, vi, 74, 79, and 126.

Wendell Warren for the photograph of him on page 119.

Curtis Willocks for his photographs of the Prospect Park Carousel, Brooklyn, New York, endpapers and page 129 top and bottom.

Index

Abilene, Kans., 43, 132
Agawam, Mass., 26, 42
Alameda, California, 134
Alberta, Canada, 124
Albion Boro Park Carousel, Albion, Pa., 58, 82
Albright, Chester E., 56, 81, 132
Allan Herschell Company, 42, 43, 50, 51, 54, 57, 63, 68, 69, 70, 72, 79, 87, 89, 126, 132, 133
Allentown, Pa., 12, 43, 86, 87–88, 131
Altoona, Pa., 56
American Carousel Museum, 126
American Merry-Go-Round and Novelty Company, 132
American Museum of Public Recreation, 66–67, 85, 134
Amusement Park Journal, 37
amusement parks
    architecture of, 46
    decline of, 47–48
    development of, 40
    early, 42
Anaheim, Calif., 123, 127
Armitage, James, 70, 131
Armitage-Herschell Company, 54, 68, 131, 132
Artistic Carousel Manufacturing Company, 82, 133
Artizan, 100
Asimov, Isaac, 125
Atlantic City, N.J., 94, 131
Auchy, Henry B., 56, 81, 132, 133
Auchy clutch, 46, 56

Balboa Park (San Diego), 21, 23, 33, 35, 46, 68, 134
Baldwin, N.Y., 23
Balmer's Pavilion, Coney Island, 131
Baltimore, Md., 97
B & B Carousel, 23
band organs, 98–101, 110, 112, 132, 133
    calliopes vs., 32–33, 102
    intricacy of, 100
    origins of, 10
    restoration, maintenance of, 100, 110
    steam-power in, 99, 100
barrel organs, 98, 99, 100
Bellefontaine, Ohio, 100

Berkeley, Calif., 52
Bickleton, Wash., 58
Binghamton, N.Y., 42, 72, 87
Black Forest (Germany), 31
Blackpool Beach (England), 73
Blue Goose, 32
Borelli, M. D., 50, 51, 56, 85
Bostock, Frank, 70
Bradbury, Ray, 11
Bradley, Dave, 70
Bradley & Kaye, 50, 70, 123
Bristol, Conn., 126, 130
Broadway Flying Horses, 77, 91
Brooklyn, N.Y., 10, 23, 30, 42, 43, 54, 70, 109, 110, 129, 131, 132, 133
Broome County, N.Y., 63, 64, 87
Buena Park, Calif., 62
Buffalo, N.Y., 100, 131
Bungarz Stage, Wagon and Carousel Works, 132
Burlington, Colo., 3, 6, 47, 101, 118, 133
Burlington, N.C., 12, 111
Bushkill Park (Easton), 14, 23, 75
Bushnell Park (Hartford), 83

calliopes, 131
    band organs vs., 102
Canada's Wonderland (Toronto), 8
Canandaigua, N.Y., 124
Carmel, Charles, 10, 49, 51, 63–64, 65, 78, 81, 84, 93, 107, 110–111, 129, 131, 132, 133, 134
Carmel, Hannah, 63
Carmel carousels, 23, 65, 83, 84, 91, 92, 126, 129
carnival circuit, 78
Carol's Carousel, 2, 4, 22, 31, 35, 40, 48, 60, 65, 88, 93, 95, 124, 126, 128, 129
carousel-building, 54–60
    factories for, 54
    production lines in, 55
    shops for, 42–43
carousels
    animals on, 5, 10, 45, 80
    banning of, 40, 132
    carvers of, 34–35
    Coney Island Style, 10, 76
    Country Fair Style, 11
    craftmanship in, 4
    electricity in, 42, 99
    emotional impact of, 11
    as fantasy machines, 1
    folklore about, 6
    foreign names for, 28
    future of, 121–126
    Golden Age of, 3, 39, 40, 134
    groups advocating preservation of, 90–91
    horse-propelled, 66, 90
    imported, 10
    language of, 24–26

in literature, 11
marathons on, 92
Maypole as ancestor of, 12
mechanisms for, 33–34, 132, 133
memorabilia related to, 104–107
merry-go-rounds vs., 10, 24
miniatures of, 106
museums for, 126
in operation today, 87
in original locations of operation, 42
origin of term, 24–26
park locations of, 135–138
Philadelphia Style, 12
primitive, 65
restoration of, 35–36, 108–119
rides related to, 30–31
rotation of, 32
steam power in, 27, 38–40, 42, 66, 68, 131
unique American style of, 10
wooden, 5, 47
Carousel Society of the Niagara Frontier, 4, 126
carousel stamps, 106
Carousel Under the Clock, 49, 50, 95
Carretta, Frank, 59, 81, 83, 84, 133, 134
Carroussel Art, 65
carvers, 58–59, 61–85
    contemporary, 104
    earliest, 62–63
    identification of, 58–60
    itinerant nature of, 59, 62–63
Causgrove, Terry, 115
Cedar Point (Sandusky), 30, 31, 32, 37, 41, 55, 87
Central Park (New York), 83
Cernigliaro, Salvatore, 59, 61, 62, 66, 68, 81, 83, 84, 97, 112, 131, 132
C. Fred Johnson Park (Johnson City), 42
Chance Manufacturing Company, 50, 54, 68, 70, 123
chariots, 32, 106, 120
    dragon, 26
    griffon, 27
    lovers, 120
Charles, Barbara, 84
Charleston, S.C., 23
Chesapeake Beach, Md., 72
Chestnut Hill (Philadelphia), 56
Chiappa Band Organ, 99
Chicago, Ill., 37, 45, 133
Children's Playground (San Francisco), 134
Cincinnati, Ohio, 131
Clarke, David, 12
Clementon Lake Amusement Park, N.J., 42
Coeur d'Alene, Idaho, 68
Colorado Springs, Colo., 110
Columbia carousels, 70
Columbus, Ohio, 74, 96
Coney Island (Brooklyn), 10, 23, 30, 42, 43, 54, 64, 70, 91, 111, 121, 131, 132, 134
Corning, N.Y., 106
Council Crest Amusement Park (Portland), 41
Crescent Park Carousel (Providence), 26, 43, 48, 76
Crommett, Gene, 48
Crystal Beach, Ontario, 49
Crystal Palace (New York), 45, 130
C. W. Parker Company, 55–56

Dallastown, Pa., 36
Daniel C. Muller and Bro., 11, 59, 66, 73, 76–78, 81, 85, 132, 134
Dare, C. W. F., 23, 58, 64–65, 66, 90, 132
Dearborn, Mich., 62, 68, 71
Deasy, Warren, 84
Death Is a Lonely Business (Bradbury), 11
DeKleist, Eugene, 100
Dentzel, Edward, 66
Dentzel, Gustav, 11, 12, 20, 45, 54, 55, 65–68, 81, 84, 106, 130, 131, 132, 133
Dentzel, Marion, 122
Dentzel, Michael, 45, 65, 130

Dentzel, William H., 11, 65–68, 77, 80, 131, 133, 134
Dentzel, William H., II, 12, 20, 66, 68
Dentzel, William H., III, 6, 122
Dentzel carousels, 15, 23, 34, 42, 43, 45, 46, 55, 59, 61, 67, 68, 70, 72, 88, 97, 112, 123, 124, 125, 127, 128, 133, 134
Denver, Colo., 13, 36, 42, 46, 56, 133
Disney, Walt, 123
Disneyland (Anaheim), 37, 123, 127
Dollywood, Pigeon Forge, Tenn., 123
Dorber, Henry, 82, 85, 133
Dorney Park (Allentown), 12, 43, 86, 87–88, 131
double tracker bars, 99–100, 101
Dreamland Park (Brooklyn), 133
"Dr. Floyd," 107
Dutch Carousel, 26
Dutch Village (Holland), 101

Easton, Pa., 14, 23, 75
Edaville Railroad (South Carver), 26
Edmonton Mall (Alberta), 124
Eisenhower, Dwight D., 43
El Dorado, 10, 121
Elitch Gardens (Denver), 13, 42, 46, 56, 133
Elizabeth II, Queen of England, 106
Elysburg, Pa., 23, 65, 83, 90, 104
Enchanted Forest (Federal Way), 16
Endicott, N.Y., 42
English Chanticleer (Allentown), 12, 88
Epcot Center (Orlando), 123
Erie, Pa., 32, 89
Euclid Beach, Cleveland, 31
Expo '86 (Vancouver), 44, 46, 111

factory paint, 36
Fairmount Park (Philadelphia), 72
Farmington, Utah, 37
Federal Way, Wash., 16
Fisherman's Wharf (San Francisco), 126
Flint, Mich., 94
Floyd L. Moreland Carousel, 106, 128
Flying Horses, 26–27
Flying Horses (Martha's Vineyard), 18, 20, 23, 65, 66
Flying Horses (Watch Hill), 22–23, 65, 72, 90
Flying Jenny, 27
flying swings, 26
flying tubs, 32
Fort George, N.Y., 133
Fried, Frederick, xi, 17–18, 100
Frontier Town Carousel, 41
Fun Forest (Seattle), 49, 51
Funland, U.S.A. (Onosko), 125

galloper, 28
Gavioli, Ludovic, 99, 132
Gavioli fairground organ, 102
Gayway (San Francisco), 46
George F. Johnson Rec Park (Binghamton), 42
George W. Johnson Park (Endicott), 42
Germantown, Pa., 66, 71, 81, 131
Gillian's Fun Deck (Ocean City), 22
Glen Echo, Md., 42, 91, 112
Glenwood, Oreg., 41
Golden Gate International Exposition (San Francisco), 46, 134
Golden Gate Park (San Francisco), 46, 68
Goldstein, Harry, 10, 82–83, 131, 132, 133, 134
Grafly, Charles, 76
Great Adventure (Jackson), 40
Great America theme parks, 50, 70
Greenfield Village Carousel (Dearborn), 62, 68, 71
Green Point, N.Y., 130
Griffith Park (Los Angeles), 84, 93, 107, 134
Gurnee, Ill., 50, 70

Hall, Gail, 4
Hartford, Conn., 83
Harton, T. M., 55, 56, 59, 77, 85
Henry Ford Museum, 62
Herschell, Allan, 11, 27, 30, 32, 51, 68, 130, 131
Herschell, Allan (grandson), 63
Herschell, Roy, 63

Herschell-Spillman carousels, 11, 21, 23, 27, 33, 35, 42, 43, 46, 52, 54, 58, 62, 64, 68, 71, 73, 87, 126, 127, 132, 133, 134
Hersheypark, Pa., 97
Highland Avenue Park (Union), 63
Highland Park (Meridian), 112
Historical Amusement Foundation, 31
Historical Crossroads Village (Flint), 94
Hofsass, Susan Price, 35, 75
Holland, Mich., 101
horses
  Dentzel, 67–68, 70, 80
  Flying, 26–27
  lead, 31
  Parker, 80
Hull, Mass., 48–49, 95
Hunting Park (Philadelphia), 55
hybrid parks, 37

Idlewild Park, (Ligonier, PA.), 94
Idora Park (Youngstown), 109
Illions, M. C., 10, 30, 45, 49, 51, 65, 70, 74, 131, 132, 134
Illions carousels, 26, 34, 74, 96, 97, 104
International Museum of Carousel Art, 4, 18, 119, 126

Jackson, N.J., 40, 85
Jacquard, Joseph Marie, 99, 130
Jacques, Charles J., Jr., 37, 84
Jantzen Beach Amusement Park (Portland), viii, ix, 46, 80, 90, 92, 112
Jantzen Beach Center (Portland), 80, 92
Johnson, George F., 87
Johnson City, N.Y., 42
Jumpers, 31

Kennywood Park (West Mifflin), 34, 42, 43, 45, 70, 125
Kent, Alexander, 131
kiddie carousels, 30
Kiddieland (Elysburg), 90
Kiddieland (Melrose Park), 81
Kiddieland Carousel, Cedar Point, 32, 55
King Arthur's Carousel, 123, 127
Kit Carson County, Colo., 6, 10, 36, 46, 49, 89, 90, 110
Knoebel, Lawrence, 90
Knoebels Amusement Resort (Elysburg), 23, 83, 90, 104
Knott's Berry Farm (Buena Park), 62
Kramer, George, 85
Kramer-Carmel Carousel, 83
Kramer's Karousel Works, 56
Kreuznach, Germany, 130

Lagoon (Farmington), 37
La Jolla, Calif., 122
Lake Compounce (Bristol), 130
Lake Lansing, Mich., 123
Lakemont Park (Altoona), 56
Lakeside Park (Denver), 36
Lakewood, Colo., 110
Largo, Md., 72
lead horses, 31
Leavenworth, Kans., 54, 79–80, 133
Leipzig, Germany, 10, 121
Leopold, Charles F., Sr., 71–72
Liberty Heights Park (Baltimore), 97
Lochman carving machine, 46–47, 55, 127, 133
Lockport, N.Y., 57
Long, Edward F., 71, 73
Long, Fielding, 71
Long, George, Jr., 35, 73, 75, 101
Long, George W., Sr., 73
Long, Lois, 73
Long, Mabel, 75
Long, Thomas V., 73, 75
Long, Uriah, 71
Long Beach, Calif., 50, 54, 70, 97
Long Branch (Syracuse), 124
Long carousels, 59
"Long Mixture," 71
Long/Muller/Denzel/Carmel, 23

Looff, Charles I. D., 10, 11, 30, 45, 48, 49, 51, 54, 55, 63–64, 68, 70, 76, 77, 78, 80, 84, 89, 91, 93, 107, 113, 115, 130, 131, 133, 134
Looff, Emma, 89
Looff Carousel (Portland), 4
Looff carousels, 11, 13, 22–23, 34, 42, 43, 48, 70, 78, 97, 116, 131, 133
Los Angeles, Calif., 84, 93, 107
Louisiana Purchase Exposition, 132
lover's tubs, 32
Luna Park (Brooklyn), 70
Luna Park (Seattle), 97
Lusse Auto Skooter, 71
Lusse family, 71

Magical Carousel Gift Shop, 128
Mangels, William F., 30, 42, 67, 70, 85, 91, 96, 131, 132, 134
Markey, Will, 36
Martha's Vineyard, Mass., 18, 20, 23, 65, 66
Maypole, 12
M. C. Illions and Sons, Carousel Works, 70, 133
Medaris, Terry, 120
Melrose Park, Ill., 81
menagerie carousels, 15, 23, 26, 33, 35, 42, 43, 45, 52, 68, 71, 72, 73, 88, 97, 112
Meridian, Miss., 112
merry-go-rounds, carousels vs., 10, 24
Middlebury, Conn., 82
Middleton Lancing Tournament (Charleston), 23
Mingei Museum of Folk Art, La Jolla, 122
Mission Beach (San Diego), 93
mixed carousels, 23, 28, 49, 84, 89, 93, 128
Molinari Barrel Organ, 100
Moore, Harriet C., 90
Moreland, Floyd L., 128
Morgantown, Ind., 31
Morris, E. Joy, 56, 72, 81, 85, 104, 132
Morton, Will, VIII, 4, 36, 110, 111
Mother Goose figures, 32
Muller, Alfred, 11, 59, 66, 73, 76–78, 81, 85, 131, 132, 134
Muller, Daniel C., 11, 41, 55, 59, 62, 66, 70, 73, 76–78, 79, 81, 85, 131, 132, 134
Muller, Henry, 76, 131
Muller animals, 14, 32, 60, 111
Murphy, Timothy, 85
Murphy/S&G carousels, 23
Museum of Early American Folk Art, x
M. Welte und Sohn, 99

Nantasket Beach, Mass., 48, 50
Nashville, Tenn., 31
Natatorium Park (Spokane), 89, 90
National Association of Amusement Parks, 134
National Carousel Association (NCA), 3, 4, 57, 61, 65, 71, 82, 90, 110, 119, 134
National Carousel Roundtable, 134
National Geographic, 110
National Historic Landmarks, 45
National Park Service, 91
National Register of Historic Places, 27, 48
Natural Mind, The (Weil), 12
Neptune Beach, Calif., 134
Newcomen, Thomas, 130
New England Carousel Museum, 126
New Philadelphia, Ohio, 73
New York, N.Y., 43, 45, 83
New York Carousel Manufacturing Company, 64, 132
New York City Common Council, 40
Niagara Instrument Company, 100
Norman & Evans, 57
North Beach (Queens), 56
North Tonawanda, N.Y., 11, 43, 50, 52, 70, 126, 132
North Tonawanda Musical Barrel Organ Factory, 100, 132
North Tonawanda Musical Instrument Works, 100
Nunley's Carousel, 23

■

Oakland, Calif., 68
Oakley, Lynda, 115
Oaks Amusement Park (Portland), 11, 32, 42, 43, 52, 68
Ocean City, Md., 68
Ocean City, N.J., 22–23, 104
Ocean Park (Santa Monica), 37
Ohio State University, 12
Old Orchard Beach, Maine, 36
Oletangy Park (Columbus), 96
Oliver, Bill, 89–90
Onosko, Tim, 125
Ontario Beach (Rochester), 72, 112
Opryland, U.S.A. (Nashville), 31
Oregon Electric Railway Museum, 41
Outdoor Amusement Industry: From the Earliest Times to the Present, The (Mangels), 85
Outhwaite, John, 73

Pacific Ocean Park (Santa Monica), 37
Pacific Palisades, N.J., 8
paint, 35–36
Palace Playland (Old Orchard Beach), 36
Panama-Pacific International Exposition (San Francisco), 46, 133, 134
Pan-American Exposition (Buffalo), 125
Paragon Park (Hull), 48–49, 50, 95
Parker, Charles Wallace, 11, 45, 57, 78–80, 131, 132, 134
Parker Carnival Supply Company, 78, 90, 94, 132, 133, 134
Parker Carry-Us-All, 27
park machines, 28
park paint, 36
parks
   amusement, see amusement parks
   hybrid, 37
   theme, 37
   traditional, 36
   trolley, 37, 40, 42, 43, 46, 47
Pen Argyl, Pa., 15, 23, 67, 124
Pennsylvania Academy of Fine Arts, 76–77
permanent machines, 28
Perron, Carol, 18, 32, 60, 63, 68, 99, 110, 111, 113, 114, 116, 128
Perron, Duane, 18, 31, 32, 60, 63, 68, 99, 110, 111, 113, 128
Philadelphia, Pa., 43, 52, 55, 76–77
Philadelphia Toboggan Company, 11, 34–35, 55, 56, 59, 67, 70, 72, 81, 84, 104, 132, 133, 134
Philipps, 132
Pictorial History of the Carousel, A (Fried), 17–18
Pittsburgh, Pa., 85, 94
Playland-at-the-Beach (San Francisco), 97
Play-Rite Music Rolls, 100
pleasure gardens, 40
P.O.P. (pay-one-price) system, 37
portable carousels, 30, 79
Port Dalhousie (St. Catherines), 13
Portland, Oreg., 4, 11, 18, 22, 28, 32, 35, 41, 42, 43, 45, 48, 52, 57, 60, 65, 68, 78, 80, 87, 88, 90, 92, 93, 95, 110, 111, 112, 124, 126, 128, 132, 134
Portland Carousel Museum, 126
prancers, 31
Price, Merrick, 26
Prior & Church, 30
Prospect Park Alliance, 110
Prospect Park Carousel, 110, 129
Providence, R.I., 43, 48
P.T.C., see Philadelphia Toboggan Company
P.T.C. #6, 3, 6, 10, 36, 46–47, 49, 56, 89, 90, 101, 110, 118, 133
P.T.C. #12, 49
P.T.C. #15, 34, 44, 46, 56, 59, 60, 106, 110, 111, 120, 133
P.T.C. #17, 37, 59, 133
P.T.C. #18, 124
P.T.C. #36, 26, 35, 73, 75, 101, 111, 127
P.T.C. #38, 12, 86, 88–89
P.T.C. #47, 97
P.T.C. #49, 42
P.T.C. #51, 13, 42
P.T.C. #61, 109
P.T.C. #62, 83

P.T.C. #72, 81
P.T.C. #75, 23, 104
P.T.C. #83, 94
P.T.C. #84, 8
P.T.C. #85, 48–49, 50, 95
Pueblo, Colo., 28, 32, 33
Pueblo City Park, 8, 28, 32, 33

Quassy Amusement Park (Middlebury), 82
Queens, N.Y., 56

racing derby, 27, 30, 30–31, 87
Razzle-Dazzle, 85
Reblitz, Art, 110
Recreation Park (Binghamton), 72
Reyes, Louise Muller, 41
ring machines, 17–23
   insurance problems and, 18, 19
   in operation currently, 23
   origin of game with, 17–18
Riverfront Park Carousel, 11, 23, 90, 118
Riverside, R.I., 54, 133
Riverside Park (Agawam), 26, 42
Riverview Park (Chicago), viii, 37, 59, 133
Rochester, N.Y., 18, 20, 72, 73, 75, 101, 111, 112, 127
Rockaway Beach, N.Y., 134
Rockaway's Playland, 134
Roehl, Harvey, 102
roller coasters, 42
rolling gondolas, 31
Rolling Hills, Calif., 74, 79
Roseland Park (Canandaigua), 124
Ross Park Zoo (Binghamton), 42
roundabouts, English, 28, 85, 133
Russell, Rosalind, 88
Ruth und Sohn band organ, 76
Rye Playland, N.Y., 30, 31, 91

St. Catherines, Ontario, 13
St. Louis Exposition, 45
Salisbury Beach, Mass., 91
S&G/Parker Carousel (Pueblo), 8, 28, 33
San Diego, Calif., 21, 33, 35, 68, 77, 81, 93
San Diego Exposition, 93
San Diego Exposition Carousel, 93, 133, 134
Sandusky, Ohio, 30, 31, 32, 37, 41, 55, 87, 127
San Francisco, Calif., 46, 68, 126, 134
San Francisco Zoo Carousel, 97
Santa Clara, Calif., 50, 70
Santa Cruz, Calif., 23, 42
Santa Cruz Beach Boardwalk, 20, 22, 23, 42
Santa Monica, Calif., 37
Savage, Frederick, 31, 40, 70, 85, 131, 132
Savage galloping mechanism, 31, 85, 132
Savage roundabout, 40
Save Our Carousel, Inc., 48
Scripture, Eliphalet, 130
Schleswig-Holstein, 76
Sea Breeze Park (Rochester), 18, 20, 26, 35, 42, 73, 75, 101, 111, 127
Seaport Village (San Diego), 77, 91
Seaside Heights, N.J., 106–107, 128
Seattle, Wash., 49, 97, 51
Seneca Park, Rochester, 101
Setyre, A. F., 130
Shelburne Museum, 127
shopping malls, carousels in, 52
Shoreline Village (Long Beach), 97
Six Flags Great Adventure (Jackson), 85
Six Flags Over Georgia, 37
Six Flags Over Texas, 134
sleighs, see chariots
Sogge, Roger, 116
Something Wicked This Way Comes (Bradbury), 11
South Carver, Mass., 26
Spillman, Edward, 68, 70
Spillman Engineering Corporation, 54, 68, 84, 107, 134
Spillman Engineering/Looff/Carmel carousel, 93
Spinning Jenny, 27
Spokane, Wash., 11, 22–23, 89, 90, 118
Sprauer, Delma and Gary, 114
standers, 31
stationary carousels, 28

steam riding gallery, 27, 68
steeplechase, 27, 30
Stein, Solomon, 10, 82–83, 132, 133
Stein & Goldstein (S&G) carousels, 28, 34, 49, 51, 60, 82–83, 90, 104, 134
Steuben Glass Company, 106
Stinson, Don, 100
Stinson band organ, 112
Stoddard, Joshua C., 131
Summit, Rol and Jo, 74, 79
Syracuse, N.Y., 124

Tacoma, Wash., 16
Tahiti, 68
Theel Manufacturing Company, 79–80, 134
theme parks, 37
Thompson, Lamarcus A., 70
Tilden Park Carousel (Oakland), 52, 68
Tilyou, George, 42
T. M. Harton Company, 79
Tokyo, Japan, 10, 121
Tonawanda Engine & Machine Company, 131
Topeka, Kans., 56
Toronto, Ontario, 8
Toshimaen Amusement Park (Tokyo), 10, 121
track machines, 27, 58
Treasure Island (San Francisco), 46, 134
Treasures From the Past, 110
Treasury of American Design, 40
Trimpers Rides (Ocean City), 42, 68
"Trip to the Moon, A," 125
trolley parks, 37, 40, 42, 43, 46, 47
Truman, Harry S., 106
Turlock, Calif., 100
Tuscora Park (New Philadelphia), 73

Union, N.Y., 42, 63, 64
U.S. Merry-Go-Round Company, 57, 65, 82
U.S. National Cathedral (Washington), 58, 65, 91
U.S. Postal Service, 106, 127

Vancouver, British Columbia, 44, 46, 111
Vaught, Diane, 111
Vinewood Park (Topeka), 56
Vogel, Louis, 89

Waldameer Park (Erie), 32, 89
Walentas, David and Jane, 109
Walt Disney World (Orlando), 123
Warren, Wendell, 119
Washington, D.C., 58, 65, 91
Watch Hill, R.I., 22–23, 27
Watkins Regional Park (Largo), 72
Watt, James, 130
Weil, Andrew, 12
Welte, Emile, 99
Wendell's Park (Fort George), 133
Weona Park (Pen Argyl), 15, 23, 124
West, Rosemary, 84
West Endicott Park (Union), 42, 63, 64
Westerly, R.I., 22
West Mifflin, Pa., 34, 42, 43, 70
West View Park (Pittsburgh), 85
W. F. Mangels Company, 56, 82
Where Angels Go, 88
Whip, 42, 85
whirligig, 28
Wichita, Kans., 50
Willamette Center (Portland), 4, 57, 78
Williams, Barbara, 84
Williams, Patrice, 85
Wonderland Pier (Ocean City), 23, 104
World Exposition (New Orleans), 68
World Forestry Center (Portland), 2, 28, 128
World of Tomorrow Fair (New York), 134
World's Columbian Exposition (Chicago), 45, 132
Wurlitzer, Rudolph, 100, 131, 133
Wurlitzer Monster Military Band Organs, 101, 110
Wyandot Lake Park (Columbus), 96
Wyandot Lake Park Carousel, 74

Youngstown, Ohio, 109

Zalar, John, 62, 83, 84, 133
Zoller, Leo, 81, 83, 84

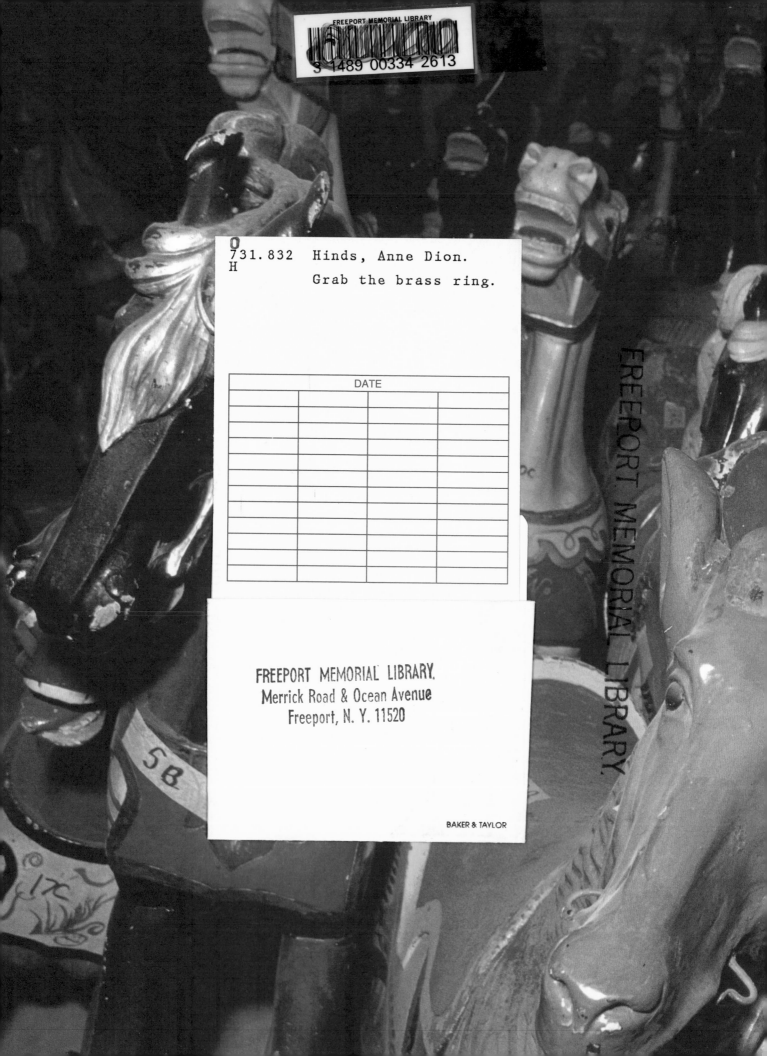